I AM THE
Bread of Life

Sr. Suzanne Toolan, Mercy Center Burlingame

I AM THE
Bread of Life

Sr. Suzanne Toolan
with Elizabeth Dossa

A Crossroad Book
The Crossroad Publishing Company
New York

The Crossroad Publishing Company
16 Penn Plaza – 481 Eighth Avenue, Suite 1550
New York, NY 10001

Grateful acknowledgement is extended to OCP Publications of Portland, Oregon, and GIA Publications, Inc., of Chicago, Illinois, for the permission to use and reprint lyrics and music herein. When lyrics or music appear on a page there is a note identifying that use as per instructions from OCP and GIA.

Printed in the United States of America on acid-free paper

The text of this book is set in 11/16 Galliard and 11/16 Triplex.

Cataloging-in-Publication Data is available from the Library of Congress
ISBN-10: 0-8245-2449-7
ISBN-13: 978-0-8245-2449-4

1 2 3 4 5 6 7 8 9 10   12 11 10 09 08 07

Contents

"I Will Sing of Your Faithfulness" was written by Sr. Suzanne Toolan after a direct commission by Roy M. Carlisle, editorial consultant and the editor for this volume. Sister often talks about how she writes best when she writes to deadline, so Roy and Liz, her coauthor, gave her a deadline for this wonderful hymn. And, of course, she came through as usual.

I Will Sing of Your Faithfulness

Refrain
I will sing, I will sing of your faithfulness and love

Psalm 16:5–6
1. My portion and my cup. It is you who hold me fast.
   For me the measuring lines have fallen on pleasant sites.
   Refrain

Lamentations 3:22b–23
2. Your mercies are not spent, your mercies are not spent.
   They are renewed each morning, so great is your faithfulness.
   Refrain

Lamentations 3:24
3. Your favors, O God, are not exhausted, are not exhausted.
   I hope in you.
   Refrain

1 Corinthians 2:9
4. Eye has not seen, nor has ear heard nor has it entered
   into our hearts what God has prepared for us.
   Refrain

I Will Sing of Your Faithfulness

Refrain

Suzanne Toolan, RSM

I will sing, I will sing of your faith - ful - ness, and love

Psalm 16:5—6

1. My por - tion and my cup. It is you who hold me fast. For

me the mea - sur - ing lines have fal - len on plea - sant sites.

Refrain

Lamentations 3:23

2. Your mer - cies are not spent, your mer - cies are not

Your mer - cies, your mer - cies, mer - cies are not

Your mer - cies, your mer - cies

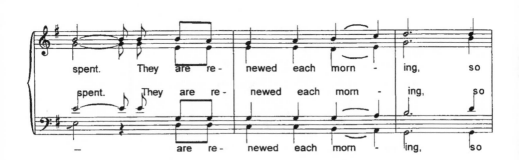

spent. They are re - newed each morn - ing, so

spent. They are re - newed each morn - ing, so

— are re - newed each morn - ing, so

great is your faith - ful - ness.

great is your faith - ful - ness.

great your faith - ful - ness.

Ref.

Lamentations 3:24

3. Your fa - vors, O God, are not ex - haus - ted, are
Your fa - vors are not ex - haus - ted, are
Your fa - vors are not ex - haus - ted, are

not ex - haus - ted. I hope in you.
not ex - haus - ted. I hope in you.
Refrain
not ex - haus - ted. I hope in you.

1 Corinthians 2:9

4. Eye has not seen, nor has ear heard nor has it

en - tered in - to our hearts what God has pre - pared for us.
Refrain

A Reflection on Writing "I Am the Bread of Life"

I've always worked best with a deadline, and a rather ordinary one was fast approaching. In March 1966, the National Catholic Music Educators' Association needed a Eucharistic hymn for their convention in San Francisco.

I had been teaching St. John's Gospel in my religion classes, and I remember being thrilled by the connection between the Eucharist and the Resurrection. In fact, the entire Gospel of John became so important in my religious development that I set many texts from that Gospel to music. And my selection for this occasion naturally fell upon John 6.

The hymn was written for the assembly to sing, but I had my high school chorale at the event as backup. In those days Roman Catholics didn't sing very well, and they needed help. I remember neither how the piece sounded nor if anyone particularly liked it.

"I Am the Bread of Life" began to be used a lot in the San Francisco Bay Area in the late 1960s. I didn't think too much about whether it was worthy music for a well-known text until I heard it sung and played not only with organ (the instrument I originally wrote for as accompaniment) but also with brass instruments. I began to be a little bit impressed by it.

As people came back from Europe and even Asia in the 1970s and 1980s, they would tell me about hearing this hymn in different countries and in different languages. I have a copy of a Slavic version, one in Korean, and, of course, one in Spanish.

I had trouble figuring out why it became popular. I know that in the Catholic Church the hymn came at the beginning of our use of the vernacular, and we didn't have much of a repertory in English. But I think that the reason it has spread is that the message of resurrection is so strong in the text.

And then there were many transformations of the music. People would come home from an event and say, "You should have heard your piece with strumming guitars. You would have hated it!" Or, "The way the group ripped through the music, you would never recognize it."

I have to admit that I have never heard "I Am the Bread of Life" without liking the group singing it. I have always been happy that people could pray with it.

"I Am the Bread of Life" is certainly not without its critics. A priest in the San Francisco Archdiocese has used the piece as an example of what should not work because it is not metric, and the range is too high and too low for congregations. There is no one more aware of this than I am!

I know the problem that some critics have with allowing the congregation to sing words that Jesus has spoken. The most recent one I have encountered is George Weigel, who calls it "that ubiquitous hymn." My question to those who think this way is, "Do you really think that the 'I' of 'I Am the Bread of Life' is being attributed to the assembly? We pray these words of Scripture. Why can we not sing this prayer?"

I have been so touched in the past few years that the hymn has been a consolation for people as they mourn the passing of family and friends. This has never ceased to make me grateful.

I'm grateful too to those who realized that the hymn could spread further than I imagined. I admit I often doubt my own work. I always bless the little freshman girl who, listening nearby as I wrote it forty years ago, liked it and caused me to save it from the wastepaper basket where I had tossed it!

SUZANNE TOOLAN, RSM

This poster/photograph of Mercy Center chapel and the lyrics to "I Am the Bread of Life" was prepared by Sr. Genemarie Beegan, RSM, and is used with permission.

Foreword

The hope of the Second Vatican Council (1962–65) was that the reform of the liturgy would bring about a renewal of the Catholic Church, which would, in turn, renew the world. This book is about the life of Sr. Suzanne Toolan, RSM, and how she has lived her life singing that vision!

Most people know Sr. Suzanne as the composer of the liturgical song "I Am the Bread of Life," sung in many settings but certainly at many Catholic funerals in the past forty years. The song is inspired — texts from John's Gospel wedded to a blessed melody. When Leonard Bernstein asked the famed music teacher Nadia Boulanger, "What makes a great musical composition?" she answered, "You do your craft, and then you *pray for the muse.*" All of us who pray with this song are certain that "I Am the Bread of Life" is touched by the greatest muse: the Spirit of God!

Written at the beginning of the postconciliar reform, this song was the first that clearly demonstrated to me that the community understood that "words matter," that the text is important. In those days, when the original text was sung at funerals, the assembly, *on its own,* began changing the masculine pronouns to feminine when this song was sung at the funeral of a woman. It was a sign that this music was different somehow — not just another song to be performed, but a text that was relevant to the prayer life of this community: The words had meaning, and the community was actively using those words to pray. Indeed, the reform of the liturgy had begun the renewal of the Church.

Elizabeth Dossa has insisted that not only should she tell the story of how "I Am the Bread of Life" came about but also the wonderful story of the composer's life. This book — *I Am the Bread of Life* — is that story.

Elizabeth Dossa is right: Pastoral music doesn't just happen. Great musicians make great music — not only composers but also the pastoral musicians who facilitate congregational participation every Sunday in every parish. Sr. Suzanne Toolan received the Jubilate Deo Award from the National Association of Pastoral Musicians not only because of her role as a composer but also because of her life-long ministry as a pastoral musician — a facilitator of participatory music. As a high school music teacher, a choir director, a musician for the Religious Sisters of Mercy, for Mercy Center in Burlingame, California, and for Taizé prayer, and even in prison music ministry, Sr. Suzanne's life is a witness that she "got it!" She has understood in the very fabric of her being that the reform of the liturgy is going to bring about the renewal of the Church, and the renewal of the Church, in turn, is going to bring about the renewal of the world. How is it going to happen? One person at a time — and this is the story of one person who dedicated her life to that task.

As you read through this text, ponder the commitment Sr. Suzanne made, the challenges she met, her flexibility to change, and her desire to go ever deeper into a spiritual encounter with the ever-present God. The text challenges our own life's journey, for in her life Sr. Suzanne has witnessed to the truth that the reform of the liturgy does indeed bring about the renewal of the Church and eventually the world. *I Am the Bread of Life* is a tribute to her living witness. It affirms that she "got it!"

THE REVEREND VIRGIL C. FUNK
President Emeritus
National Association of Pastoral Musicians
St. Patrick's Day, 2007

How to Read This Book

I Am the Bread of Life offers readers the opportunity to follow Sr. Suzanne Toolan's remarkable journey as a Sister of Mercy in a series of biographical essays or to sit at her feet and learn from her wisdom about music, liturgical reform, and life in the Spirit.

Note ornament: In nine numbered essays (one, two, etc.) you will find Sr. Suzanne's thoughts on Music and Mystery, Silence, Liturgy, Ritual, Belief, Celebrations, Prayer, Thirst for God, and Symbols. An ornament of eighth notes begins each essay and is also found in the running heads at the top of each page. We invite you to learn about music and spirituality from this humble and wise woman.

Cross ornament: From her earliest days as a young novice to her senior position as an elder in her community, Sr. Suzanne's remarkable personal journey is chronicled in ten winsome and engaging biographical essays. Although these essays are not numbered, they are clearly marked in the table of contents beginning with the first, which is titled "A Reluctant Star is Born." These essays are marked by the Sister of Mercy cross, an ornament that begins each essay and also appears in a modified form in the running heads.

Additional practical material: In addition readers will find six shorter essays on topics of a practical nature. These brief pieces are in shaded boxes throughout the book or they can easily be found listed in the table of contents.

Mercy Center, Burlingame, California

ONE

The Work of
Music and Mystery

*In the end, religious life is about worship and the positive
benefits worship brings to the world and its maker.*

— Jo Ann Kay McNamara, *Sisters in Arms**

♫ Most of us have had profound experiences of liturgy,
a time when heaven and earth are knit tightly together.
The Word is clearly proclaimed, heartfelt voices join warmly
in the hymn, and each person seems attentive to the mystery
taking place. It could be a packed Christmas Eve Mass or a
Sunday in Ordinary Time with half the congregation in sweat
outfits.

Suzanne Toolan, RSM, a Sister of Mercy, has centered her
life around these communal experiences of God almost since
she walked in the door of the Mercy Motherhouse in 1950.
She's modeled good liturgy, insisting gently on its principles,
and taught others how to pray, how to sing, and how to put
together the puzzle of a reverent celebration. In the process,
she has captured the hearts of other musicians, liturgists, retreatants, students, and even prisoners at San Quentin State
Prison.

Her principles have arisen naturally from a sensibility tuned
to what others need to draw closer to God. She doesn't

---

*Jo Ann Kay McNamara, *Sisters in Arms* (Cambridge, MA: Harvard University Press,
1996), 637.

preach ideas; her intuitions and observations flow from her and the way she lives her life quite naturally. They are captured here from her conversations, comments from those she has touched, and a retelling of her experiences. What follows is not an intellectual exercise but a passing on of wisdom.

People are drawn most to her humility and reticence. "She listens, looks directly in the eyes of the person who is speaking with her," said the late Nancy Bannister, director of the Western office of the National Association of Pastoral Musicians. "She does that powerfully human thing of being present. That is what liturgy is about — all of us being present to the presence of God."

This modest musician is tall, now with a cap of short white hair, often slightly disheveled, as if it must find its own way to order. Her face breaks quickly from solemn impassiveness to a brilliance radiating from her gray eyes and laughing smile. She laughs frequently, out of her sense for the charming and comical lying below the ordinary.

Sr. Suzanne is able to do a disappearing act while directing people to the experience of God, especially through liturgy and music. She facilitates or points the way to the mystery. This is not to say that she doesn't have opinions. She has a firm aesthetic and theology of liturgy that guides the choice of flowers in the sanctuary, the robes worn by the participants in the Good Friday service, and, of course, the songs selected.

She disappears because she has a special grace, an innate shyness that deflects attention from herself. The congregation becomes absorbed in the beauty of the ritual that flows smoothly from start to finish. Just as teenage students in her chorale years ago fell in love with music by Vittoria and Bach, the congregation is drawn face-to-face with musical purity.

She's not all perfection. She has patterns from childhood that those who work with her today recognize with a sigh.

Her natural sister, also named Suzanne, remembers one of those patterns: "The night before class I did all my home-work. She would never do hers. On the streetcar to school she would take out an envelope and do the assignments." In the years since, Sr. Suzanne often has taken out an envelope and composed a stirring piece of music or even written parts and a melody during a homily. Those of us who labor at our work are envious of her amazing talent.

With a lifetime devoted to liturgy, she has much to pass on in accumulated observations and attitudes rather than rules. This journey together is an attempt to capture a glimpse of that spirit.

A Reluctant Star Is Born

People most successful in religious life don't fit into a mold. They understand how to draw on religious life to be themselves. —John Renke, choirmaster of San Francisco's Schola Cantorum

The tall, thin teenager shrank into her seat on her first day at Hollywood High School. Clumps of students loitered in the hallways in their sweater sets. Gloria Ernestine Toolan slid under the social radar, flattened herself into what she hoped was obscurity, and continued on her own way. She felt so insignificant in her new school that years later she was surprised to find her name listed in the graduating class. She hadn't been a ghost.

In her own mind, Gloria had been forced to move to this raw area of the country, where new residents flocked to the mild climate and houses were replacing orange groves. In Lansing, Michigan, where she grew up, the winters might have been cold, but the nest of family and friends was cozy. That her parents had dreamed of living in California was irrelevant. She didn't want to move, but no amount of resistance or pouting had helped. She was here to finish high school.

She didn't make friends at the school. No one spoke to her, and she was not about to begin the conversation herself. The boys wore jeans, which she thought was ridiculous since she couldn't see any farms for miles. In 1944, the other students were future starlets and producers, ambitious for their own careers.

Like many of her classmates, Gloria became a star. But on her stage, modesty and inner life were key elements. There were no

24

dressing rooms or bright lights or full orchestras. Candlelight and pews set the scene.

There were similarities: she changed her name, for thirty years she wore what some might consider a costume, and she has published tapes and CDs of her work. She is famous, maybe not on the big screen or in *Time* magazine, but anyone, Catholic or Protestant, who has sung hymns in church in the last forty years has felt her influence.

Her childhood, where she had been surrounded by family, parish, and school, had been blissfully insular. Her father's Irish-Catholic heritage determined that Gloria, her older sisters, Patricia, Mary Louise, and Suzanne, and her younger brother, Jack, would go to Lansing's Holy Cross School staffed by the Sisters of Mercy.

She plodded along in elementary school because she wasn't interested. She didn't even like her teachers very much; she spent time looking out the window and thinking about recess. The Sisters were demanding and strict. She was interested in playing in the neighborhood

The park across the street from home offered space to play and to roller-skate, and the future composer was a fine roller skater, according to her own estimation. Her grandfather flooded the backyard during the winter and tried to make it into a skating rink, which the children appreciated even if the ice never got quite hard enough.

But her body was wired for music. As a youngster, Gloria saw a piano in a store; her heart raced. She felt strangely confident. Boldly she went up to the instrument, climbed up on the piano bench, and tried a few chords. The keys felt good to her small hands, and she played a little more.

The clerk came up, "Miss," he said sternly," we can't have you playing this piano."

Little Miss Toolan obediently climbed down, but she had made a great discovery. She didn't know how, but she would need to play around with those notes. She could make wonderful sounds; she already knew how to create harmony.

The day was remarkable partly because Gloria was painfully shy. She was very close to her sisters, especially her next oldest sister who was christened Suzanne. The older Suzanne, a self-described "eager beaver" in school, was her playmate and confidant. The two, always together, played jacks, skated, and ran freely around the neighborhood. Along with their sister Mary Louise, they formed a trio and sang "Love's Old Sweet Song" and other well-worn favorites to treat their paternal grandmother. Gloria could sing any part, and Grandmother loved to entertain and show off her granddaughters to her guests.

Gloria and her older sister also shared the shyness. Their mother, Ada, a hard-working, quiet woman, was sensitive to the need for the refinement of art for her children. She knew that her daughters needed "bringing out" of their stiffness, so she sent the two to a dramatic arts class. Perhaps the girls would learn to speak up to an audience of strangers, to sing and dance freely across the stage.

"The class didn't succeed," reported the much amused composer and singer years later. "The teacher typecast us as wooden soldiers!" The stiff little actress grew into an adult who was most comfortable with her back to any audience.

Ada was pleased to see her daughter's interest in music that day in the music store, but since the Toolans didn't have a piano, she sent Gloria and her older sister to the Mercy convent for lessons. "I spent most of my time looking at the clock, seeing if my time was up yet," confessed the composer.

"I hated practicing, but I loved music. I was a very lazy little girl. What held me back was that I could play things by ear. After my next oldest sister, Suzanne, had her lesson with the nun, she would come out and say, 'You are going to get it today. She knows you can't read music.' "

Of course, the slacker managed to play well enough. She looks impishly cheerful about her childhood resistance. She didn't practice because she didn't have to. Her talent allowed her to quietly disregard the rules, a situation that repeated itself throughout her life.

But their next music teacher, although blind, was very observant. She told Gloria sternly after she had gotten through her lesson, "You have not practiced. There is no use in having piano lessons." Then she would call the girls' mother on the phone, but Gloria, also observant, noticed that the teacher held the receiver down when she called.

Gloria's talent must have been obvious because the music lessons continued, with or without practicing. By seventh grade, she was playing the organ in church for several Masses and earning a quarter a Mass. Absentmindedly, she would stuff the money into her skirt pockets to be discovered by her mother when the bills floated up to the surface of the wash water.

The opportunities for music multiplied. She spent time dreaming, imagining, and writing, as she puts it, "drippy little things. I went through a very holy period with saccharine texts in high school."

She remembered her organ-playing experiences with a shudder. "In high school, I used to play and sing morning Mass at 6:30 a.m. at the cathedral in Lansing. We would have three Masses in a row. The trick was to sing it just as fast as you could — you know, gloriainexcelsisdeo. There was no participation in those days. No one else would sing, and the priest was trying to get through it fast. It was a liturgical nightmare," she said.

As unsatisfying as they looked to her later, these experiences of liturgy still drew her. As a young child she had attended the entire Holy Saturday services in the Lansing cathedral. "I remember that I walked there in the early morning, and I was practically the only one in church. It began at 5:00 a.m. I devoured the whole thing—the readings, the Eucharist, all in Latin," she remembered. The sense of ceremony and music were part of her even then.

In 1944, her life in Lansing came to an agonizing end for a teenager. Her father, especially, dreamed of palm trees, bungalows, and sunshine that never stopped. He and his wife had visited California several times and decided to move the family to Hollywood. After they had sold the house and were ready to move, he had a stroke; the move was delayed for a month until he was stable. Then in October, their mother drove the girls and their brother, Jack, to California. Their father followed soon after.

Gloria felt rudely uprooted from her beloved St. Mary's High School in Lansing where she had taken college courses and had a cozy group of friends. She and her girlfriends adored the Sisters of Charity nuns, hung around with them after school, helped clean the sacristy, and sneaked sips of altar wine. Feeling very privileged, she had a key to the school that she used to let her friends in on weekends when they were downtown and wanted to use the bathroom. She thought about joining the Sisters of Charity, but the thought was transient.

The teenaged Gloria sulked in the backseat all the way across the country, according to her own account. "I was such a brat," she remembered. "My mother had to drive. She would say, pointing out the window, 'Look at this, it's so beautiful.' I would ignore her."

Hollywood had tall palm trees but, in those days, little glitter. It felt like a small town, but for a Michigan native there was nothing familiar about the place—the dry air and arid hillsides dominated by the beacon of the Hollywood sign could have been on the moon.

The Toolans moved to a Spanish-style house on Hollywood Boulevard, five blocks from Grauman's Chinese Theater. She lived here with her family during her last year of high school and throughout college. The family entered a sunny, casual culture, with its three-story elegance, in a smogless Los Angeles basin with orange trees nearby; the film industry was beginning to discover its powerful images.

Choosing first the familiarity of a Catholic school, Gloria went to Corvallis High School, a Catholic girls' school over the hill in the San Fernando Valley. In her three-day stay at Corvallis High, "I was a fish out of water," she said. "Everyone knew everyone else. It seemed cold."

Deciding to abandon the Catholic school and go to Hollywood High closer to home, she learned that the public school was "the devil's playground." Corvallis Principal Sr. Mary Thornton, a Sacred Heart of Mary Sister, pursed her lips when she learned that this malcontent young woman, ill at ease and yet determined, was dropping out of her school for a secular one. She warned Gloria not to leave but apparently didn't try to make her feel welcome at Corvallis.

At Hollywood High, Gloria coped by plunging into an area of comfort — music. She took two music classes and was enrolled in a half-day schedule designed as a vocational program for students with little interest in academics. She could leave at noon to go home to practice; she didn't have much in common with the other students. Music consumed her time and her emotions.

"I began to study with organist Richard Keyes Biggs, a well-regarded organist and choir director in the area. My goal was to play organ professionally. He asked almost right away if I would be his assistant at his church, St. Paul's, next to the old St. John's Military Academy [which was run by the Sisters of Mercy]."

In 1945 she was a good Catholic girl devoted to her music. The thought of a religious vocation tempted her. She could have become a Sister of Charity. She could have joined the Immaculate Heart of Mary Sisters who ran Immaculate Heart College, which she attended after high school. Strong, forward-thinking women, the IHMs also ran elementary and high schools in Los Angeles. Her sisters Patricia and Mary Louise would enter the Sisters of Mercy.

"My father would have been happy if all five of us entered religious life. He must have had a positive experience with nuns as a child. He named my sister Patricia after a Sr. Patricia he had had in school. As an owner of a deli and a liquor store, he got the nuns in Lansing things that were hard to get during the war — butter and coffee."

But Gloria was not ready to commit herself to religious life, even with family encouragement. For several years, she couldn't make up her mind.

She and her biological sister Suzanne went to Immaculate Heart College together, taking the street car. The college was small, and the music program not difficult. Although, during this last year of World War II, soldier friends from Michigan would visit the family, sleeping on the floor, and eating a good meal or two, Gloria wasn't attracted to the idea of marriage. It didn't seem the right path for her.

More important even than the organ lessons for her inner life and her later vocation was her work with Lucianne Gourdon Biggs, Richard Biggs's wife. Gloria accompanied Lucianne's choruses at Villa Cabrini Academy in Burbank. "I grew to love choral music," says Sr. Suzanne. "It was so much more than joining voices. It is such a vehicle of joining people's spirits. The voice is the most human of instruments — to join people on that level, to be a part of that is wonderful."

But she was willing to give up that love for another life.

Seeing a Garden in a Dream

To ignore a dream is to ignore a letter from God.

—The Talmud

At age twenty-two, Gloria hovered between choices. Especially in the pre–Vatican II Church, religious life was undeniably a higher calling than that of a lay musician. For her, as for thousands of young women in the 1940s and 1950s, the heavy black habits with veils and coifs that tightly framed nuns' faces were familiar costumes; the girls had been taught by Sisters. Life in a convent seemed a holy alternative to life behind the kitchen sink. They heard God's call clearly then as young women, even though a good number either were found "not suitable" for community life or later realized structured group living and eating in silence was not what they wanted.

Perhaps God used Gloria's tentativeness. After high school her organ teacher, Richard Keyes Biggs, called Gloria's parents and suggested she spend concentrated time in practicing the organ. She didn't do well with that unstructured time. "It was a terrible year," she said. "Undisciplined. Terrible." Years later she grimaced at the memory. "I've never been good at practicing. I went through the motions. It was a year of indecision."

She lived at home while attending Immaculate Heart College majoring in public-school music education and studying piano with faculty member Franz Darvis. She admitted that college was easy for her; she probably should have gone to a college with a larger music program.

31

As part of her training at IHC, she even returned to the detested Hollywood High as a student teacher to study under the excellent Miss Jeter. The budding student taught Carol Burnett in her music appreciation class.

Gloria was gaining a reputation for expertise. During this time she was organist and choirmaster at St. Ambrose Church in Los Angeles. Fr. O'Toole relied on this talented student for her competence and musical knowledge, even asking her what organ he should buy for the church.

"Certainly not an electric organ," she said, knowing that was what he wanted. "I think it would be lovely if you would buy a Casavant, made by a Canadian organ builder." She confessed later that her knowledge was actually limited; she knew Richard Biggs had a Casavant, so she thought it must be the best. The priest looked aghast at the idea of a purchase of a pipe organ for his small church, but he didn't comment further.

Two of Gloria's older sisters, Mary Louise and Patricia, had already entered the Sisters of Mercy when Gloria was in college. She traveled up to Burlingame from Los Angeles for a "visiting Sunday," once a month when family visiting was allowed, and was drawn to the place itself.

The forty-acre campus housed Sisters from postulants to the professed in the imposing Motherhouse, built in 1931, with its chapel tower and the double front doors. Gloria probably wandered the grounds, the green lawns, under the old oaks, up to the rose-brick Kohl Mansion, which served as the high school building. Off limits to the public, the acreage was a private oasis nestled in Burlingame's residential community. Most Burlingame residents were unaware of its presence.

She insists her next step had nothing to do with her sisters being in the Mercy community. She had a powerful dream, the only one of her life that has directed a major decision.

"In the dream, it was a beautiful day, and there was, at that time, a beautiful flower bed in front of the Mercy Motherhouse. It was a lush, lush green, and I just knew from that dream that I should come here." As she told it, her long slim fingers moved gracefully, recreating the memory out of the air.

"When I was a student at Immaculate Heart College, I wanted to go to the Immaculate Hearts. I liked them very much, but after the dream," Sr. Suzanne's voice trails off, then she continues, "I can see the spot as I am walking up the hill to the college. I said to myself, 'The reason you want to become an IHM was that you want to teach music in college.' After the dream, it didn't seem like a good enough reason to enter there."

She knew she wanted religious life, but which community? When? The dream of lush beauty brought Gloria firmly to the Mercy Motherhouse door. She felt it as the clear call she had been waiting for. She tried to explain, "It wasn't the garden exactly. It was just that I knew I should enter the Sisters of Mercy from the dream."

Gloria's mother told her, "Don't pack your music. If you do, you are saying, 'I've already determined what I want to do.'" As she remembered Ada's cautions to her, Sr. Suzanne smiled at her mother's wisdom.

Her mother had sensed a truth gathered from two of her daughters' earlier entry into the community: even the uncloistered Sisters of Mercy, all of them teachers and nurses, did not make their own choices in the early 1950s. They went where they were assigned by their superior and did what they were told. For the sake of community, they conformed to the good of the whole.

The mission of the Sisters of Mercy was education of women and children and care of the sick, especially the poor. Catherine McAuley hadn't mentioned music when she founded the order in Dublin, Ireland, in 1831.

Gloria went back to Fr. O'Toole for a reference to the Sisters of Mercy. He was her parish priest, and she needed his recommendation. Although he also must have been pleased in some ways, Pastor O'Toole stubbornly expressed deep disappointment with her request. He had had other plans for her.

Telling the story recently with barely contained laughter, she mimed his reaction, bending at her desk, holding her head gloomily in her hand. "'I have ordered a Casavant,' he said to me with great resignation and then glumly added, 'I had such high hopes for you being our music person and our housekeeper.'"

Politely declining the invitation to be a priest's housekeeper, Gloria wrote to the Mother General Mary Thomasine Kelly to apply for entrance. "I want to work out my salvation and work for the salvation of *men,*" she wrote. She laughed at herself years later when her perspective had broadened, saying "Such bad theology. As if it were just *men* I was working on, and the phrase 'working out my salvation' is such an ego-centered and limited theology."

Mother General quickly wrote back accepting the young woman. "I was so introverted, I don't think they would have let me in today," she commented years later with typical self-deprecation. "If they hadn't known the family, they would have asked more questions."

She wasn't to bring clothes; those would be provided. The convent long johns, vests with long sleeves, cotton underdrawers to the knees, and corsets would be given to her the day she entered.

As Gloria put black-laced shoes, comb, brush, pen and pencil in her suitcase in the summer of 1950, she knew she would begin a radically different life. She had surprised her family with her determination to become a Sister of Mercy. Her sister Mary Louise had entered the Mercy convent in February of 1948 and Patricia a year later. Their firmly Irish-Catholic father, Ernest, had been pleased. When their mother, Ada, learned that yet another daughter wanted to enter, she said, "I don't even have much faith and to think that three of my daughters would become nuns!"

Leaving her mother, she flew up from Los Angeles to San Francisco, her first plane ride. "Diana Petz and I arrived together in the early morning. It was a Saturday and what you did in the convent on Saturday was cleaning. They were busy cleaning, so they sent us down to greater Burlingame to eat our last lunch out of the convent. We sat at the train station looking longingly at those trains, wishing we could go home."

Fourteen young women entered the Sisters of Mercy Burlingame Region on the Feast of the Visitation, July 2, 1950. A virtual flood of vocations, they represented part of the unprecedented numbers of young women who entered religious life during the 1950s and early 1960s in the United States.

Despite her earlier anxiety, Gloria felt at home almost immediately. "We expected silence, discipline, and getting up early, but we were given freedom the first few days. The plums on the property needed picking, so we were sent out to pick plums. We had a good time together."

The property was studded with California oaks in the hills of Burlingame. A stream ran along the north side, and carefully cultivated gardens and a small orchard provided fruits and vegetables. A shrewd Mother Superior had bought the Tudor mansion and the wooded land around it from Frederick Kohl's mistress in 1924 for $230,000. By 1950, the Mercys no longer used the mansion as their convent Motherhouse; a four-story convent had been built down the hill, and the mansion was given over to the high school, which had opened in 1932. In the midst of a prosperous Burlingame, which housed white-collar workers from San Francisco, the religious community was set apart. Only Sisters' families, who were allowed to visit once a month, and Mercy High School students and parents came to the fenced campus. The iron gates between the pink pillars at Adeline and Hoover were closed at 6:00 p.m. No local parishioners came to the Gothic Motherhouse chapel.

The postulants expected to be removed from the world. Although the Sisters of Mercy sponsored a high school, taught in a number of elementary schools, and ran hospitals, their rule, explained in *The Guide for Religious Called the Sisters of Mercy,* clearly focused on the pursuit of interior perfection. They read from the guide every day for years. It instructed that reaching perfection had many facets: service to the poor, tending the sick, cultivation of union and charity among the Sisters, maintenance of the spirit of poverty, chastity, and obedience. Interior prayer and silence were to be practiced. The introduction to the monastic routine of silence, prayers, and work was gradual during the first week.

As an antidote to potential problems, the guide directed them to keep a guard over their senses, "lest the enemy who is constantly on the watch should penetrate through these avenues to their souls and tarnish in the least the purity of their hearts."* Humility and mortification, not of the body but "of the senses, imaginations and caprices," were part of the rule. Should this direction not include the sensual beauty of music, those delicious sounds used to glorify God? Was the garden in the dream to be pruned and disciplined? Would the young composer have to offer this up?

The world receded. "We put on the postulant outfit, a long black dress with a little veil," she remembered. "We wore collars and a little band around the headpiece, which we took turns washing, starching, and ironing with flat irons. Rita May, an energetic and zealous girl from Buffalo, New York, was famous for using such thick starch we would prick our fingers trying the get the collars on. Everyone was charitable, loving but not gushy. I ate the whole thing up."

Silence and discipline began to take hold. The Great Silence began each evening when the postulants retired to their dormitory rooms at 9:00 p.m. They arose at 5:00 a.m. to a Sister knocking on the door saying, "Lord Jesus, preserve us in peace." To which the reply was a usually sleepy, "Amen." Prayers and Mass were followed

---

Guide for Religious, rev. 1962, 54.

by breakfast, which was silent. The monastic routine was designed to move the young postulants — the median age of her group was twenty-one — out of their family life to the life of community and prayer.

For some, the silence and solitude was unbearable. Some left, often feeling defeated by what they thought was a lack of vocation. One in her group left after four days. Another was asked to leave because she used her prayer time to scribble notes to her boyfriend. Gloria thrived. With her friendly smile and gentle shyness, she was immediately liked by the other young women. She didn't mind the structure or the quiet, and she wasn't really deprived of what she most loved.

The second day she was in the convent, the novice director wisely asked her to send for her music. "It was probably a stupid thing not to have brought it. They knew I had just finished school and was a music major. Our community has always been very practical. I love that phrase from Angeles Arriens: 'walking the mystical path with practical feet.' That's what we have done."

An uncertain note sounded at her first meeting with Sr. Marguerite Buchanan. Marguerite — a violinist, among her other talents — had entered six months after Sr. Suzanne, and the Superior felt Suzanne might be able to help her feel at home.

Sr. Marguerite told the story with relish. "The night I entered, Sr. Mary Eleanor wanted to be sure someone talked to me during recreation, so she asked Suzanne to do that, maybe because I played the violin. After we talked for a while, I said to her, 'Is this almost over?' She doesn't ever let me forget that!"

Not an auspicious start to what became a lifelong friendship that resulted in creative projects from giving retreats to opening Mercy Center.

TWO

Silence as Personal Practice

Silence is going beyond words and thought. God is nothing like what we say he is or what we imagine he is.

— Anthony de Mello, SJ

♫ Silence is a natural element for Sr. Suzanne, perhaps the primary element, even before music. It gives her spiritual oxygen. She creates silence with the ring of a bell at early morning meditation in the Motherhouse chapel, bringing others with her into the depths of communal quiet. Often, in ordinary speech, thoughtful silences separate her sentences. She's at ease with introducing more silence into the liturgy.

For many of us, silence is raw and uncomfortable. It's the space when nothing is happening, when someone has dropped her music or forgotten his lines. It's the moment in a group when no one can think of what to say next, and a glacial stillness paralyzes us. We want words, any words to restore a feeling of normalcy, to keep the rhythm going.

But words are a convention that can restrict us. We wrestle with trying to say the right thing, with building bridges. We want to pick the appropriate texts for services, find the right words for a prayer, or say the consoling thing. "Words, words, words, I'm so sick of words," complains Eliza Doolitle in *My Fair Lady*. She's sick of learning the words appropriate for a lady, and she wishes Henry Higgens would recognize the emotions behind the dry words.

Silence can be a healing disengagement from social effort, from trying to present a particular persona, from thinking of the next word. In *Sitting Still: An Encounter with Christian Zen* Patricia Clifford writes of how stillness led her into a Mercy Center retreat: "When I looked back over my life, I found that the most memorable moments were of times I was sitting still — listening to the rustle of leaves or the splash of a mountain stream. Only when I stopped did I become something more than the sum of my doing."* As anyone who works in the Church knows, the job brings no guarantee of knowing that we are more than the sum of our doing. The obligations of planning liturgies, choosing music, rehearsing a choir, working with a pastor can seem even heavier because the purpose is so "holy."

Sr. Suzanne doesn't preach about silence. Although from time to time groups of pastoral musicians will pressure her to give a workshop on liturgy, she doesn't do it willingly, even though she feels that in order to be involved in music and liturgies, one needs rich spiritual reserves. When she taught students in chorale, she taught by the example of her passionate love of music. Now she models what she's learned about silence over fifty years.

Finding silence is a natural talent for her, but realizing it and helping others find it has been a theme that has developed gradually in her life. At one time, Sr. Suzanne was conducting two choral groups, teaching a full load of music classes, starting up Mercy Center as a retreat center, as well as composing and creating liturgies. Rushing around the campus, copying music, and making phone calls to presenters pulled her apart. One of her friends said, "I was really afraid she would work herself to death."

---

*Patricia Clifford, *Sitting Still: An Encounter with Christian Zen* (Mahwah, NJ: Paulist Press, 1994), 7.

In *The Shattered Lantern,* Ron Rolheiser observes that one of the obstructions to contemplation today is "an unbridled restlessness" that allows no room for not doing, for interior space. "Being filled, yet unfulfilled, comes from being without deep interiority. When there is never time or space to stand behind our own lives and look reflectively at them, then the pressures and distractions of life simply consume us to the point where we lose control over our lives."* Perhaps we don't take more time for silence because we are afraid of it. Social beings, we are reassured by the noise of others around us, by the drone of the talk on the television, by radio chatter when we drive. Sr. Suzanne's immersion in music and prayer was built on a talent for silence nurtured by religious life.

For some in religious life, silence is a burden to be accepted; for Sr. Suzanne it has been a nourishing element. "Silence is written into our lives as nuns," she said. "We have daily silent prayer, even if it is distracted." She laughed a laugh that said, "Don't take us too seriously. We're human. We wiggle."

As there are fewer religious, we have fewer reminders of this pattern of prayer, quiet, and retreat. We have to work harder to claim it for ourselves. A friend with young children who worked as a hospice volunteer told me she had to quilt for several weeks before she could take on a patient and a family. She needed the steady quiet of pushing the needle through the cloth to settle her down before she could be a source of nourishment for those facing death.

The power of silence to allow disengagement is a first step toward this interiority. Think of times in your life you have walked out a door, leaving a loud party and a deafening band behind. The cool physical relief is abrupt. Your neck, back,

---

*Ronald Rolheiser, *The Shattered Lantern* (New York: Crossroad, 2001), 50.

and even ears relax. You can hear your own voice again. Your heart slows down. The nourishment of a lowered stress level rushes over you.

The lyrics of one of Sr. Suzanne's most evocative hymns brings a hush with it when read or sung:

> *Stilled and quiet is my soul.*
> *In God's presence I take my rest.* *

As Sr. Suzanne instinctively feels, silence, beyond being a relaxing state, is an opportunity, an opening. Her ease with silence permeates her music and is part of the fabric of liturgy and prayer. Taizé prayer with its periods of communal stillness has been a constant in her life since 1983.

When she entered the Mercy community in 1950, the Great Silence began each evening at bedtime and lasted through prayers, Mass, and breakfast the next day. It wasn't easy for everyone. "Recollection brings freedom of spirit," proclaimed *The Guide for Religious Called the Sisters of Mercy,* from which every novice had to read daily until the mid-1960s. A quote from founder Catherine McAuley was posted on the way to the Sisters' dining room: "Silence produces recollection and recollection produces prayer. Prayer leads to union with God." Perhaps the quote made the silence during meals more bearable.

Ideally, when Sisters passed each other in the hallway during the day, each cast down her eyes, avoiding personal contact; "custody of the eyes" was important and talk was only about essentials. "This didn't always match reality," Sr. Suzanne said with an impish glint in her eyes. "Sometimes we had to go into the hall broom closet to give each other messages. We weren't above sharing some gossip, either."

---

*"Stilled and Quiet," GIA copyright © 1966.

But unless there was a special feast day, Sisters preserved silence during the day in the convent except during recreation periods when they came together in the community room after supper with knitting, handwork and sewing to enjoy group conversation.

"You got to know the liturgical calendar very well — when the Saints' days were — so you could talk," Sr. Suzanne said with a laugh. "Once you got used to it, the silence wasn't difficult. I thought it was nice, actually, but I'm an introvert."

She remembered two blood sisters who entered the community together. "Sr. Ursula worked in a hospital, and Sr. St. James lived here in the convent. Every year Ursula would come to the Motherhouse and its beautiful grounds for her vacation. We would look outside and see the two sisters sitting on a bench, arms folded, saying nothing. We knew they knew what each other was thinking. They didn't need to talk."

Silence can be a medium in which relationships flourish, as did Sisters Ursula and St. James's friendship, but people can't easily drop out of the clatter of busy lives into a state of silence. "Today we are so super active, so busy with our bodies and in our minds that we can't come abruptly to silence," said Sr. Suzanne. For many, Taizé prayer has been a way in to stillness, a setting where cell phones and fidgeting disappear.

Sr. Suzanne doesn't have formulas. She doesn't claim to know The Way. She gives suggestions, hints, and examples, which she says modestly, "You can take or leave if they don't help you." She has insights and passions, which she shares. On a recent day of prayer Suzanne began with Jesuit Anthony de Mello's observation on silence: "Any way to God has to go through silence."

She offers some basic techniques for finding this silence.

Find a time of day that works for you. We nuns used to have to pray at 5:00 a.m., and for many of us that was a time to fall asleep.

1. Quiet the body. Sit comfortably. Make sure your feet touch the floor. Straighten your back.

2. Quiet the mind. Use a technique that is comfortable for you.

   Lectio divina: Read a Scripture passage slowly out loud. Use the word or words that attract you as the focus for your silent prayer.

   Count your breath: This frequently used meditative technique helps focus the mind. Fr. Tom Hand, SJ (who led the East-West meditation program at Mercy Center for twenty years), taught it as part of his meditation. It requires intense concentration. I knew a contemplative who was on number one for years. When he got to two, he was so excited; he had to go back to one!

   Centering Prayer: This technique taught by Trappists Fr. Thomas Keating and Fr. Basil Pennington goes through the preliminaries of a relationship with God — acquaintance, friendliness, and friendship, to union of life, resting in God. You chose a word that symbolizes your intention of being in God's presence but doesn't have other associations for you. A word in another language is good. You introduce that word, but when you find yourself gnawing on a thought, you go back to your word with the intention of being in God's presence.

"Sr. Marguerite Buchanan and I introduced Centering Prayer to San Quentin State Prison about eight years ago.

In our prayer with the men there, we are very aware of the men who are new. They fidget and squirm during the twenty minute period. If they return the next week to the Centering Prayer session, they begin to welcome the silence amid the terrible chaos of prison life."

Sr. Suzanne doesn't think religious have any claim to being "better" at silence than lay people, especially since Vatican II. "It is so surprising that laypeople have come to silence and have gone further in it than we have in contemplative prayer," she said. "Fr. Thomas Keating said when he first started with Centering Prayer he was following through with what Vatican II had asked for in sharing their practices with the world. The monks never realized how laypeople would take to it, very easily and very quickly."

For everyone, clergy, religious, layperson, or prisoner, silence is our most intense response to God. "Sometimes words come forth," said Sr. Suzanne. "Sometimes the mystery is too much for words, so there is music. Sometimes it is too much for music; then there is silence."

EXERCISES FOR SILENCE

Sr. Suzanne often uses the following steps to help others find inner quiet on retreat days:

Understand

Come to the realization that words and ideas are inadequate. Meditate on this reality. Recall each idea you have of God and say to yourself, "God is more unlike this than like it. God is far beyond this and far better than this."

Look

Look at some nature scene or at an object. Don't look for anything sensational. Just look as if you are seeing it for the first time.

Listen

Listen to all the sounds around you. If possible, avoid putting names to the sounds. Realize that each sound is really composed of many sounds. Don't look for anything sensational. Just listen to those sounds as if you are hearing them for the first time in your life.

Scripture

Recall your favorite sentence of Jesus from the New Testament. Repeat it to yourself. Imagine Jesus is standing in front of you, and he addresses those words to you. Don't dwell too much on the meaning of the words. Resist the temptation to react. Don't say anything, and don't respond in any way. Let the words reverberate and resound within you. When you cannot contain it anymore, respond to Jesus.

A variation of this exercise is to become silent first. Then recall a sentence from Scripture or ask someone to read it to you. Those words of Scripture will be etched in your heart, and they will deepen your silence. They may take on a meaning that is quite beyond the power of words to express.

— Anthony de Mello, Argus Communications, 1985

738   I Am the Bread of Life

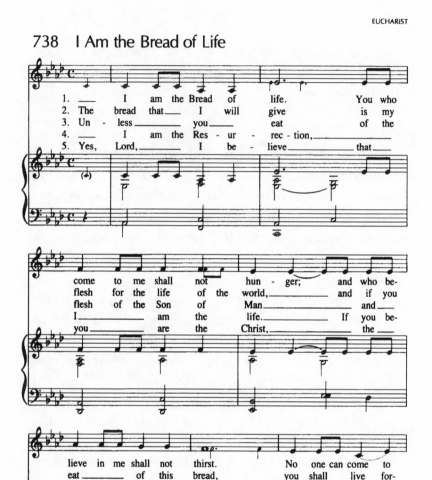

1. ___ I am the Bread of life. You who come to me shall not hun - ger; and who believe in me shall not thirst. No one can come to
2. The bread that ___ I will give is my flesh for the life of the world, ___ and if you eat ___ of this bread, you shall live for-
3. Un - less ___ you eat of the flesh of the Son of Man ___ and ___ drink ___ of his blood, and drink ___ of his
4. ___ I am the Res - ur - rec - tion, ___ I ___ am the life. ___ If you be - lieve ___ in ___ me, e - ven though you
5. Yes, Lord, ___ I be - lieve ___ that ___ you ___ are the Christ, ___ the ___ Son ___ of ___ God, Who ___ have ___

The Toolan sisters in full habit at Mercy Center, from left to right, Patricia, Gloria, Mary Louise.

The Stays of Habit

St. Thomas tells us that [perfection] consists in a prompt and determined will to do at once and cheerfully whatever we know to be the will of God. Now, we have no difficulty in discovering this, for our Rules and Superior are to us the voice of God.
— The Guide for the Religious Called Sisters of Mercy (1962), 3

Sitting in her office chair in casual sandals and soft pink blouse and skirt in 2006, Sr. Suzanne spoke of her early convent years with a charming openness and humor. Her voice had a musical lilt when she talked, and her laugh of pure delightedness in a funny story was accompanied by a small explosive snicker and a radiant smile. Experience lined her face at seventy-eight — all the moments her mouth moved with the words for her students, her eyes opened wide in encouragement, the times she famously "scrunched up" her face at a wrong note — all were stored there. She generously shared her old programs, letters from students, and photos, almost as if she didn't want to make too much of their preciousness. She held a picture of herself in a long black habit from the 1950s. In this shot, she is in front of a choral group, one arm reaching up high as if for the note, her face hidden.

The habit, which she had accepted as a part of the package of community, spoke loudly. The distinctive uniform announced the Sisters' defined life with its sense of call and purpose. Its traditional long black serge with the tight white coif over her head, rigid plastic guimpe over her front and shoulders along with bone stays

48

in a corset signified restrictions of action as well as definition of her role.

The habit posed some practical problems for conducting music. The starched parts of the coif rubbing against the guimpe (the white bib that sat on top of the black tunic) made so much noise Sr. Suzanne couldn't hear very well. The long sleeves got in the way of sweeping gestures, a liability that just seemed to her part of life at the time.

She accepted the restrictions as part of what gave her life definition. Her theology was narrowly Catholic. "I had such a righteous faith," said Sr. Suzanne. "I passed judgment on a lot of people. I was a pious Sister." Talking about those years, she admitted she was very scrupulous, regularly reading materials like "The Pope Speaks" published by *Our Sunday Visitor.* At that time in the early 1950s, she was a different person from the Sister who admired Protestant hymns in the 1960s and welcomed Buddhists to Mercy Center in the 1980s.

Was this pious young woman entering a life different from the torturous convent life one reads about by women who entered a community and left? Yes and no. It was structured, hierarchical, and probably oppressive. The Sisters of Mercy were a community of women who worked in the world, but they were in fact kept separate from laity in their search for holiness. Mercys could only go out in twos, didn't drive cars, lived only in large convents. It was a pre–Vatican II monastic life.

Entering as a postulant in 1950, Gloria also sensed that extraordinary graces were part of these lives. She had seen the Sister teachers in her high school having fun together, being part of a close group. She was tempted to join the Sisters of Charity after high school, and later the Immaculate Hearts looked attractive. In her years of living at home during college, she longed to make a commitment, to decide.

More importantly, Christ was a presence in her life, calling her to a life of community and prayer. Her dream of the garden came as a compelling message to commit herself to the Sisters of Mercy.

Tremendous revolutions were in the wings for the Church in the 1950s, waiting for the right moment to break through. Liturgy, religious life, and the role of the laity were all about to be transformed. Sr. Suzanne and her work would act as yeast, gradually changing the shape of liturgy and prayer in her Mercy community and then beyond.

Her sisters Mary Louise and Patricia had entered the Sisters of Mercy in 1948 and 1949, respectively. After six months as a postulant, each was accepted into the community as a novice. Although the Superior gave the novice her new name at her reception of the veil, the young woman could request three choices. When she received her veil, the then Gloria listed Humiliata and Barbara as possibilities, but her first choice was her biological sister Suzanne's name because "she was the angel of the family." Gloria was delighted, then, to be given Suzanne as her new name. In a family shuffle, her sister Mary Louise took the name Mary Gloria and her other sister, Patricia, adopted their father's name, becoming Mary Ernest.

Being received as a novice with a new name was only a step. There were two years of formation, which meant being molded into religious life, before her first profession. It was an intense time of learning to pray, understanding the vows, studying theology, and becoming part of a community. Sr. Suzanne liked the interior work.

The novice director, Sr. Mary Eleanor Cahill, was responsible for introducing the young women to convent life, checking on their progress in regular meetings or conferences. She respected their spiritual life and tried to find books appropriate for each novice. Sr. Suzanne had done spiritual reading, but she felt she didn't have a developed spirituality. How did you really find your way to God regularly? What kind of prayer is best?

Sr. Mary Eleanor gave Sr. Suzanne *In the Likeness of Christ* by Edward Leen, CSSp, and the classic *The Imitation of Christ* by Thomas à Kempis. Eagerly she threw herself into the reading.

At the same time, she was discontented and managed subtle rebellion. Her habit had a corset with bone stays for proper restriction. The novice removed the stays from her corset; she was slim anyway, and they poked and prodded her unnecessarily. That she got away with it was typical. She moved in the direction of reform and change, but slowly, in ways that came to seem obvious improvements.

After two years of formation Sr. Suzanne prostrated herself on a January day with the other ten young women (three had already left the group) in the ornate Mercy chapel, pronouncing the vows of poverty, chastity, obedience, and a promise, particular to the Sisters of Mercy, to serve the poor. Her mother, Ada, and, of course, her sisters were present at this ceremony of her first vows. Ada sat separate from the nuns behind the screen at the edge of the Sisters' stalls with the rest of the families. Her father had died before Sr. Suzanne entered.

"I had arrived at heaven's door. It was a wonderful feeling of bliss," said Sr. Suzanne. Here in the dark wood chapel, the beauty of the Latin words and ritual filled her with peace. She was sure this was the right path. Any doubts or indecision had vanished.

The formation years prepared her for convent life, which followed a strict, monastic schedule in the 1950s. The Motherhouse was a pattern of rules and predictable routines from rising at 5:00 a.m. to retiring to bedrooms at 9:00 p.m. Most Sisters worked a more-than-full day of either hospital duty or teaching in one of the elementary schools staffed by the Mercys or in one of the two high schools they ran.

Routine, order, and sometimes exhaustion prevailed. "In the 1950s, we lived a monastic community life with demanding prayer routines and also felt the increasing pressures of min-istry — extracurricular activities, meetings at night, schoolwork," remembered Sr. Barbara Moran, who entered the community with Sr. Suzanne.

"But every rule we had was meant for a reason," said Sr. Suzanne. "Silence was meant for interior recollection. Not talking at meals was meant to keep you recollected. The rules were not meant for repression. The Sisters of Mercy were never meant to be a contem-plative community. Catherine McAuley's idea was that our life is centered in serving the poor, as 'walking nuns.' To keep that desire clear, silence would nourish us."

One difficulty for Sr. Suzanne was that she found the instructions on prayer incomplete. "I was waiting for them to do a better job of teaching us how to pray," she remembered. "Then there were *not,"* she paused on the word for emphasis, "many helps available. In those days, I don't think they knew them. We would sit at 5:25 a.m. with a book of meditations in front of us. It wasn't an ideal time to pray. You were tired and sleepy. Such simple things we can do now would have helped so much — like body awareness, watching the breath. Centering Prayer, which teaches you to let go of everything, would have helped. We weren't given these techniques then."

She wasn't to find more satisfying patterns of prayer for herself for twenty years.

The young novice struggled with some practical skills. "The novice director was astute in many ways. She understood people," said Sr. Suzanne. "She knew I have never been able to delegate. To this day, I cannot delegate." Her voice rose in mock horror. "In the novitiate you had house duties. [There was no hired staff.] The day after I got my white veil, she put me in charge of the refectory, to teach me to delegate.

"It didn't do me any good. I did everything myself. On first-class days (feast days or special holidays) we had white tablecloths, and once there was a hole in the tablecloth. I have never been able to sew, but of course I wouldn't ask anyone else to help. The next first-class day they pulled out the tablecloths, and one was horribly mended with a Turkish towel! The novice director knew immediately who had mended it. I got in a little trouble."

"The little trouble" was most probably asking pardon from the novice director on her knees, a common penitential practice in those days. Sr. Suzanne endured it, but her delegation skills didn't improve.

The Sisters didn't spend all their time on their knees or in a classroom. The Guide outlined a nightly recreation period that began with saying a "Hail Mary" while standing. Then the group sat together at long tables, sewing, listening to records, and talking, although private conversations were discouraged. Cliques were frowned on, but of course Sisters who entered together or worked together had a special bond. The goal was building a loving community of women who supported each other and talked freely in a group.

Feast days were very special. Celebrations included talking all day and lots of eating. As time went on, recreation on feast days grew into parties with hilarious skits, recitations of poetry, and Sr. Suzanne's own musical impressions of Sisters.

"We spent a lot of time together in chapel," explained Sr. Suzanne. "We knew how we each walked, genuflected, and sat. One of us would throw herself into her stall. Another would slip in demurely."

On the spot at feast-day parties Sr. Suzanne would sit at the piano and begin to improvise. The delighted Sisters would laugh and clap as they recognized the person Sr. Suzanne was evoking in music — short bounces for Sr. Assumpta Murray, a gliding graceful tune for Sr. LaSallette Trevillyan. Her observant improvisations were one of her great contributions of fun to community life.

The Mother General assigned her to teaching piano lessons as part of the Mercy School of Music headed by Sr. Mary de Chantal

Perz. She would drag herself up the hill to the lessons and sit uncomfortably in the room with a ten-year-old who hadn't practiced. She tried not to show it, but she was bored with the piece she had heard hundreds of times.

"I hated it," said Sr. Suzanne. "I'm a real introvert, and they say that introverts have real trouble with one-on-one, but with an audience they are fine. The bigger the audience, the better for me."

Finding that audience took a little time. The emphasis in community was on fitting in, not on distinguishing yourself as an individual, according to archivist Sr. Marilyn Gouailhardou. And Sr. Suzanne didn't want to attract attention. "She didn't, and doesn't, like to make waves," observed Sr. Marilyn.

Another problem in addition to the unsatisfying instruction in prayer was that the young musician shuddered at the music available to the Sisters and the Church in general.

She was slowly forming the community's musical tastes. "Before Suzanne, every convent had an organist," said Sr. Marilyn. "We had a music tradition, which included things like a 'Litany of the Blessed Mother,' which sounded to me like a polka, but she moved us forward. The words to the hymns from *St. Gregory's Hymnal* and *The Mount Mary Hymnal* were Victorian and pious. She changed that."

In the late 1950s, Sr. Suzanne had a brainstorm, one of the most important ideas of her life. She went to Mother Cyril Driscoll one morning. She didn't make it sound like a big decision. The Mercys already had a tradition of music — organists at the convents, a music school, and a choral group at the high school.

"I asked if I could have a special group of novices," she said, "as a schola." They could practice together and sing at liturgies. She promised they would fit in the practices and not take time away from studies.

She didn't have to wait for an answer. Mother Cyril agreed easily to her request, not dreaming that the Burlingame Mercys would become known for their excellent singing; four-part harmony would run in their blood. The fame of her compositions would touch the Burlingame community.

Sr. Suzanne felt led to make the request. The opportunity for musical excellence presented itself, and she took it, not thinking about where it would lead. "I am very pragmatic," Sr. Suzanne said. "I love to compose for an occasion with a group that I know. I find it hard to sit down and compose without a goal." Over the years, knowing the voices and skills of her choral groups was a great advantage in her composing.

"Although we didn't have a lot of practice time, they sounded good," she remembered fifty years later. "We did three- and four-part harmony, and I was composing at this time. I was terribly busy, too busy. I was teaching at Mercy High Schools in Burlingame and San Francisco. I was giving private piano and organ lessons, which I hated. In 1960, Sr. de Chantal finally realized that I hated piano teaching and released me. That was such a wonderful thing!"

The schola was an extracurricular activity for the novices who qualified. People had to audition, and with space at a premium with so many novices, the singers had to migrate in a search for rehearsal space.

"Space was so tight before we built the Russell College building, that one year we had the schola in the community room with Sr. St. James working away with her sewing machine whirring in the corner," remembered Suzanne. "We had music in the basement lumber room with only one light bulb burning in the ceiling. Another year we sang in the storeroom behind the Coolock Hall stage because the grand piano was there.

"It was fun. The postulants had gossip scoops we professed sisters never knew. For instance, we are getting a new carpet in the chapel! And the color! Our practice times were lovely, refreshing times for them and for me."

"The novices were immersed in study," said Sr. Suzanne. "Recently they have said that music got them through difficult times.

They got to know Scripture through the music. It could have happened with any director, but the singing opened them up. In the 1960s, we felt very confined and crowded. Music was a wonderful time of breaking out." For those young women, many of whom had entered the Sisters of Mercy after high school and found themselves almost suffocated by the regimen of the novitiate, Sr. Suzanne's rehearsals were a great escape. "Formality was the rule in the convent," said one-time novice Lorraine Paul. "We were so studious, focused on theology studies. There was nothing but joyfulness about singing with Suzanne. We used to sing schola songs when we did the dishes. We began to know good music because of her modeling."

Rey Friel, who was in the convent with Suzanne from 1963 to 1983, found that Sr. Suzanne's classes allowed her to bear convent life. "I don't think I could have survived those years without [schola]," Rey said. "Convent life was very repressive — silence, isolation, and solitude. You were ripped away from everything familiar, but to sing was a new way of being. It was a source of joy."

Although Sr. Suzanne felt too busy, the years that followed were years when she wrote song after song for her groups for high school graduations, special Masses, and conferences.

One day, listening to her chorale reverberate in the high school's Great Hall, she had another idea. These sounds should be preserved. Why not a record? She decided to make a recording of the schola and the high school chorale together, both for the singers and for use in other churches. In early 1970, she called Dan Odum, a baritone in her high school Gilbert and Sullivan productions, who was a conductor and a recording engineer. Dan, who was very fond of Sr. Suzanne and thought her musicianship "amazing," quickly accepted.

One evening he hung the microphones in the balcony of the Motherhouse chapel where the choruses filed in to sing. Then Sr. Suzanne stood in front of the group and conducted, as if it were any ordinary day. They sang the pieces once. The girls and novices knew the selections, her compositions, perfectly. They were disciplined, able singers. There was no rehearsal. The young women sang, crisply and cleanly, in an ethereal chorus. "It was excellent sound quality," said Dan. "A big part was the quality of the choir and the ambiance of the chapel. I did very little editing."

The *Living Spirit* album was produced from that one session, certainly an astonishing accomplishment. In the 1990s, it was reproduced as a CD.

The composer was also honing her expertise in liturgy. From 1953 to 1963 she taught liturgy at the College of Our Lady of Mercy, the college for the novices on the Mercy campus. She and Sr. Jacqueline Crouch, a brilliant English teacher and innovative thinker, organized liturgical conferences for the Sisters in the 1950s. By November 1960, the Worship in Our Life conference — which dealt with covenant, psalms, *ecclesia,* and the laity's share in Christ's priesthood—saw 225 Sisters in attendance. Liturgy was a primary concern for the community.

The Mercy community annals contain an interesting note concerning the Worship in Our Life conference. At the sung dialogue Mass in 1960 celebrated by Fr. Robert Hayburn, director of music for the Archdiocese of San Francisco, permission was given for an offertory procession by Sisters. Sisters were allowed to bring up the bread and wine for the first time in their community Mass. If participation by Sisters in the Mass required permission, the changes made by Vatican II for the whole Church a few years later would be felt as dramatic.

THREE

The Natural Act of Liturgy

To celebrate the liturgy means to do the action or perform the sign in such a way that its full meaning and impact shine forth in clear and compelling fashion. Since liturgical signs are vehicles of communication and instruments of faith, they must be simple and comprehensible. Since they are directed to fellow human beings, they must be humanly attractive. They must be meaningful and appealing to the body of worshipers or they will fail to stir up faith and people will fail to worship the Father.

—*Music in Catholic Worship,* United States Conference
of Catholic Bishops' Committee on the Liturgy, 1972

♫ "You know I am not a liturgist," said Sr. Suzanne, her long fingers briefly conducting her thought in the air, returning to rest on her lap. She sat in her office off the Motherhouse chapel, the corner room in shadow on this winter afternoon. There was evidence of a liturgist's work being done: the upright piano on which she composed, a plaster Christ Child from the Christmas crèche perched on her desk. The deep closet was stacked with choral pieces, orange Taizé prayer books, and tapes of her compositions. An accumulation of fifty years of liturgical experience gently contradicted her.

The liturgy at the Sisters of Mercy Motherhouse has long been known as beautifully prayer-filled, as experiences at convents and monasteries often can be. The difference is that

58

in Burlingame there has been one liturgist over the years and through the many changes in liturgical form. A composer and teacher, Sr. Suzanne has fashioned the services for the Mercy community and the larger congregation with great care, guided by her pastoral sense and her aesthetic convictions.

She spoke about liturgy not as if it were a subject of study, but a loved and thoughtful habit. "Liturgy is a natural act. It's the 'work of the people,' doing what comes naturally as a group of people," she said. "Fr. Tom Hand, SJ [who led the East-West meditation program at Mercy Center for twenty years], used to say, 'In meditation, you let your whole being take its natural course, one of movement toward God.' In liturgy as a community, we need to let ourselves take the natural course, which will be different at different times and which has to move past distractions."

From instinct and experience, Sr. Suzanne has honed wisdom over the years that can help others to tune in to a truly pastoral liturgy. Her key themes are focusing this "natural course" and minimizing distractions for the congregation. Both require thoughtful preparation and discipline.

Sr. Suzanne's early experience of liturgy had not been a particularly "natural" one. As a talented teenager, she played the organ at Masses in the cathedral in Lansing, Michigan. A series of services began at 6:30 a.m. following the same lickety-split routine in Latin with the congregation obediently paging the prayer book and the priest mumbling, as if the Mass were a kind of charm. She saw the services later as "awful," but they propelled her to search for a different kind of public prayer.

The Sunday Mass at the Mercy Motherhouse in Burlingame is a gem of an hour. The light in the Gothic chapel is warm and dim, filtering through the high stained-glass windows, and sound is softened by the expanse of beige carpet. Sr. Suzanne often begins by going to the microphone and rehearsing a few lines of a new song, leading with her pure, small soprano and demonstrating the tone levels with her hand like the good choirmaster she is. She slides onto the piano bench; her hands resting on the keys for a moment, her head slightly bent, and then she begins the gathering song.

She presides, weaving the elements together into a pattern of quiet reverence that reflects her own deeply prayerful presence. She has chosen the songs, the readings, arranged the flowers, selected the altar vessels, asked visiting musicians to play, and invited the priest. Simplicity rules, as if the elements of the Mass have burned down to their essence over the years for her.

Her ease and understanding comes from study, but she has been immersed in a life that has given her the right tools: eager singers, encouragement from her leadership and a patterned prayer life. She and the Mercy community worked together in making the liturgy more "natural" before Vatican II. In the 1950s and 60s, Sisters attended the University of Notre Dame for summer courses in liturgy. Sr. Suzanne remembered that they brought back "a whole new way to look at this ancient sacred act. The manner of celebration was modeled there. The emphasis was on meaningful participation." She recalled year after year of liturgical institutes at the Motherhouse organized by Sr. Jacqueline Crouch, an intrepid and brilliant English teacher who produced new ideas at breakfast before anyone else was awake.

Even though the Sisters of Mercy were not radical in changing their habit or their governing structure, Sr. Suzanne led them in making changes in liturgy and music. She had a talent for "operating under the radar of leadership," as one Sister said, "and getting away with it."

Adding music to the Mass was a first step, and from music other changes unfolded. "The liturgy here in the 1950s was fairly advanced," Sr. Suzanne remembered. "We jumped when we could get a priest to do a dialogue Mass or *missa recitata,* allowing a liturgical conversation between the presider and the congregation. In the 1960s and 1970s, Mother Eucharia Malone thought the sisters should have a good experience of liturgy once a week, so composer Fr. John Olivier, music director at St. Patrick's Seminary, came on Saturdays. We had a good homily at least once a week!"

Sr. Suzanne began writing music for her schola to sing at those Masses. "I always had an interested group of Sisters who loved to sing. The rest of the community would join us. We sang whenever we could. I can remember sitting in a room in the novitiate, now Mercy Center offices. We would be waiting for the novice director to come in. Sometimes we had a long wait. I taught people three-part songs, and we just sang away."

Focused participation has always been Sr. Suzanne's key concern for her flock, whether they are Sisters, parishioners, Taizé attendees, or retreatants at Mercy Center. She thinks about every liturgy she prepares in the context of the Church year.

She summarized the basic ingredients: "The classic movements of liturgy are *adoration, thanksgiving, petition,* and *reparation.* One seems more dominant depending on the season. We can stand in awe before God. Sometimes we come in thanksgiving when we are conscious of the overwhelming goodness of God. In times of disaster, we can stand in petition, pleading before God. Of course we can ask for forgiveness when we feel a need to say we are sorry."

She has woven these elements together thousands of times. They are no longer ideas, but part of her own natural movements toward God. "In every Eucharist, there are elements of each of these stances," she continued. "During Lent, which is the great retreat of the Church year, we focus more on preparation for new life. The penitential aspect, once the primary focus, is still evident. We dim the lights. We take away the fringe elements so we can concentrate more — no Gloria, no elaborate flowers. The altar is stripped down, the vestments are purple, but the more important part of Lent is its preparation for Easter. It is the planting season of the year, the time of interior work, quiet preparation.

"In worship as social beings, our corporate being takes its natural stance, often one of thanksgiving and awe. We let ourselves as a community move toward God. This process is a natural flow, reflecting the seasons of the physical world, and bringing our experience of nature to liturgy." She paused and looked on her desk for something.

"I just read an article which Sr. Pat [Ryan] found about new research with the Hubble telescope, which has unprecedented views of space." Her eyes lit up at the thought, but she gave up her search for the article itself. The idea astonished her. "It focused on a spot as big as a dime, only for the astronomers to discover that these dime-like dots hold galaxies! Galaxies! There is such hugeness, yet also the intimacy of God who sustains my every breath. Liturgy enables us to bring what is in nature, the whole wonder of creation to worship."

Nature also can be chaotic. Sr. Suzanne strives for flow, not sudden jolts in her own liturgies. The service at the Mercy chapel has attracted a regular congregation because of its smooth, reflective quiet that allows the Word, the music, and the outstanding homilies to shine. Coming to Eucharist is an actual experience of "the source and summit of all liturgy," as Vatican II's Constitution on the Sacred Liturgy described it. The surrounding community gathers: Sisters, neighbors, school alumni, retreatants. A few small children run up the aisle or bang the kneelers. But Sr. Suzanne is aware that the "natural flow" of God's people is bigger than even an ideal, prayerful atmosphere.

She remembered when the point was brought home to her. "A group of us were coming back from a liturgical institute years ago where the experience had been wonderful. We stopped at a church in the city where the congregation was old people, distracted teenagers, screaming kids. There were smells of food on people's clothes and people chattering away. Our Church is a mixture that can drive you crazy as a liturgist. My first thought was, 'This is not it!' And then I thought, 'This *is* the reality — a motley group that is a wonderful symbol of who we are as Church. This is the reality of the Body of Christ that comes together and worships.'"

Throughout her conversation ran the theme that the beautiful and the holy are inextricably bound together. The holy makes the motley beautiful. A liturgy is not about lace and chanting by great choirs, although those are very nice, she admitted with a wistful smile. True liturgy is about leading the congregation to the Real Presence.

Sr. Suzanne has firm convictions about what liturgy is not. Liturgy is a form but not a performance, she cautioned. Her wisdom comes out of her experience as a musician who has loved the perfection of soaring four-part harmony. The experience of beauty can be ecstatic, as anyone who has heard cathedral choirs at a midnight Mass or the tenor filling an Agnus Dei with longing.

But the Body of Christ is often not orderly or aesthetically pleasing. "When people from the community first came to

Mass here at the Motherhouse chapel twenty-five years ago," she remembered, "someone had a retarded child who sang whenever we sang. She sang off-key and not in rhythm, but I thought it was so beautiful. Many people were irritated. It did spoil what we were singing, but it also perfected what we were singing."

If music in the liturgy is not a performance, neither is the role of the priest primarily to be center stage, maintained Sr. Suzanne. "The priest is a presider, not a star. Sometimes they go on and on, fond of their own voices," she said.

Her reaction recalls Thomas Day's abhorrence of the "host" priest in his acerbic *Why Catholics Can't Sing*. A genial personality, this priest conceives of his role as a jolly welcomer and "good guy," in the process directing attention to himself and away from the community's relationship to God. The priest is a convener, a facilitator of the mystical body of Christ, important for his role, not his personality.

If liturgy is not a priestly performance, neither is it supposed to be primarily good "theater." But don't we need drama to express our deepest feelings? "Smells and bells," brocade cassocks, and candlelight all help. The funeral Mass of Pope John Paul II with its dramatic red carpet and the simple casket, the cardinals in red, the processions, the chanting is a recent example of a dramatic liturgy that allowed the world to grieve and feel the farewell.

But at that funeral, the primary purpose was not to glorify the choir or the priests officiating. In the midst of magnificence, the focus was to celebrate John Paul's passage into the presence of God and to reinforce the community of believers. Local parishes don't usually have to worry about being carried away by magnificence. They just need to stay focused on the simplest elements of the rite, which will allow the experience of God for the community.

Sr. Suzanne has a deep faith based on her experience that if you open the door and get out of the way, God will enter. Unclutter, allow silence, provide singable songs, encourage people to hear themselves sing.

"The liturgist is a choreographer who gets out of the way so the worshipers are not conscious of the movements. I like what Martha Graham once said: 'You spend years training muscles in the studio, so you can forget it all on stage. Then art takes over.' The liturgist should train, study, and pray so that in coming to create a liturgy all the elements are there but invisible. Even the liturgy itself is not the important thing — it is a form, a vessel."

During a recent Lent, her setting of the Motherhouse chapel was eloquent. A simple branching cactus sat in front of the altar. It said, "This is a desert time. There is space, silence, and sparseness until Easter breaks forth."

Liturgy as a natural act is created through intense preparation. The seams and wires should be invisible. The readers need to be familiar with their texts, the microphones tested, the chalice ready. Then there is the letting go. When the gathering song begins, the Spirit takes over.

Behind the Music Stand

There were a lot of people who had a spiritual experience at Mercy that is still a part of them. The Mercys seemed so relevant. After I had Sr. Suzanne in high school, I thought of her and the other Sisters of Mercy as people who lived their faith as a rich tradition. Suzanne was part of the beauty of it.

—Catherine Murphy
Mercy High School Burlingame alumna

"Life at the convent could be routine, but there was always something new going on at school," said Sr. Suzanne. As prayerful as she was, she was drawn by new projects and the flurry of new ideas.

School Sisters had a window into changing American culture. Through their students, Sr. Suzanne and other teachers had some exposure first to Elvis Presley, then the Beatles and the tie-dye culture of hippies. They staffed drama and choral rehearsals and chaperoned dances, duties that both allowed and required them to be out at night, putting together scenery or checking on the proper distance between dance partners.

Sr. Suzanne began teaching at the high school on the Burlingame campus as a second-year novice. She first assisted choral director Ralph Laris, but she took over the class after a year. "Principal Sr. Mary Martin wanted to save money, so she gave me the class," she said, neglecting to mention her love and obvious talent for teaching. And Mr. Laris, as good as he might have been, was not a Sister. At first she was understandably nervous. One day a casual observer gave her some good advice.

66

"During my first year, a painter named Mr. Terheyden was working on the back of the auditorium [Great Hall] during class. At the end of the class, he came up to me and said in heavily accented English, 'You must show them you luff them, you luff them!' I said, I'll think about that.

"He came back a year later, observed the class, probably while painting another wall, and said, 'You luff them now!'" The memory brought much laughter from Sr. Suzanne.

She did show them she "luffed them" over the years in ways that Mr. Terheyden couldn't have guessed. She insists she wasn't good at class management. Sr. Mary Lois Corporandy assigned student grades for her at first and made seating charts for the bus when the girls went on trips.

"Assigning seats was something I would never do—would never want to do!" Sr. Suzanne said emphatically. That amount of order seemed excessive to her. Her classroom discipline flowed from the music itself.

She began with the basics for the freshmen. "What I would do first with a group is to let them hear harmony; I would play chords so they could hear that. They liked to hear simple things like 'Let Us Break Bread Together'—chord, chord.

"With kids there is a lot of imitating of sounds. I can't tolerate swooping up to the note. They learned not to do that. I love really crisp, clean sounds."

Several students remember that in spite of her sense that it was the music that drew in the girls, she had firm control of the classes as a teacher. She won the students quickly with the energy of her conducting.

"She would stand on her toes, stretch her hands up," remembered Sue Kneer who sang in chorale from 1967 to 1970. "She would purse her lips and bring in her hands. You could sense from her hands the emotion and the level of sound she was looking for. She would smile from ear to ear when you did it right. There was something about her personality that made us all want to please her and do our best for her." Her gentleness attracted the girls, and her passion for the music was contagious; she did whatever it took to produce the music well.

"She had no tolerance for people disturbing her class. She was very firm on that. If another section was rehearsing, you were quiet," said high school alumna Rey Friel.

"Class was geared to performances and concerts. It was understood that you paid attention. She gave you a look that you knew meant to settle down," said Mary Williamson Gadson, who graduated in 1979. "If you moved, you were caught. She looked at you. She had high expectations and set the bar high."

She wasn't just teaching the girls music in high school; she was introducing them to the whole tradition of excellence. "I remember a musicologist saying, 'If something is worth doing, it's worth doing poorly,'" said Sr. Suzanne. "It is better to do a great composer poorly than a shabby composer well. I really believe that. It is true that just giving kids the exposure to what is good is what matters."

In the early 1970s, Sr. Suzanne and Sr. Marguerite Buchanan — school principal, violinist, and adventurous thinker — grew to be fast friends. Sr. Marguerite's office was in the front of the mansion, which is the core of the high school building. Sr. Suzanne's chorus would rehearse across the hall in the wood-paneled Great Hall. "The singing was so beautiful," remembered Sr. Marguerite. "It was nourishment for the soul."

She needed nourishment. A year or two earlier, San Francisco State College had rioted. Mercy was in disarray, as students even in a Catholic girls' school reflected discontent with authority. Sr. Marguerite did not renew the contracts of five teachers who encouraged the students to rebel against a variety of rules. As a result of her decision, the student body officers resigned. The sky didn't fall in. "We got along without them," said Sr. Marguerite. The school quieted down the next year.

In this time of radical student discontent, Sr. Suzanne also had the duty of teaching religion. The religion department made some creative adaptations to the students' general restlessness. The teachers, all Sisters, gave the students an innovative spiritual inventory. They then classified the students by their attitudes toward faith. There were the "spirit girls," the "social girls," and the "atheists." Sr. Suzanne was assigned to the atheists. She managed with a simple technique: letting them gripe about religion for several weeks. "When they got tired of that, I taught them about responding to the sacred in all kinds of things."

The Mercy community was living through a time of internal siege as well. After Vatican II, Sisters began leaving in large groups. "We would get a half sheet, 'Please pray for _____ who is being dispensed from vows.' In 1969, we got a sheet with sixteen or seventeen names on it," said Sr. Marilyn Gouailhardou. The number entering the convent slowed to a trickle, and some years stopped altogether.

Sr. Suzanne had been in community for twenty years. Getting up in the morning and finding that several friends were leaving saddened her, but she had a solid group around her. Sr. Marguerite and Sr. Pat Ryan formed the stable core. Sr. Suzanne was committed to her work, her girls, and her own spirituality. Vatican II had given her the freedom to write music in English. "I Am the Bread of Life" was being sung all over the world.

"It was more disturbing for young people in the 1970s," she said, "and I wasn't that young then. [She was in her forties.] A lot of us felt very solidly here. We would feel very sad when some of our friends would go, but I felt very rooted in the community."

Her music expressed a deep longing for God. She wrote of being fed through the Bread of Life; spiritual thirst was a theme of "Living Waters." Her music reflected a contemplative spirituality that she would more fully realize through the influence of Fr. Tom Hand, SJ, and the music of Taizé prayer.

Changes affected the community. In 1966, the Sisters of Mercy had adopted the mid-calf length, dark blue habit and short veil. They began to be able to choose their ministries, so Sisters began dropping out of their hospitals and schools into a variety of roles — social work, advocacy for the poor, and spiritual direction.

Even though Sr. Suzanne felt rooted in the community, she began to feel discontent with the pattern of institutional living in the Motherhouse. She was a leader in shifting the pattern. Each Sister lived in a small bedroom cell with central bathrooms and a "community room" where gathering was permitted. Sisters Suzanne, Marguerite, Pat Ryan, and Marie de Lourdes went to the leadership and said that living in a group of seventy-eight women was what Sr. Suzanne today calls "crazy." At the time, they termed such rigid institutional living "not helpful" for their community growth.

They succeeded in creating several smaller living groups. The Sisters who taught at the high school had bedrooms on the second and third floor of what is now Mercy Center. They shared a community room (living room), which is now the Cypress Room on the first floor. Naming it Montsalvat, or "mount of salvation" from the Parsifal legend, they continued to live in a group for ten years, creating a living pattern that the whole Mercy community gradually adopted.

Sr. Suzanne and her own biological sister, Sr. Pat, then the drama teacher, joined together in producing musicals at the high school. They began with Gilbert and Sullivan, using the small, high stage at one end of the Great Hall. A formidable personality with high artistic standards, Sr. Pat was always the big-sister disciplinarian, strict and exacting about everything that Suzanne was relaxed about. Together they produced *The Pirates of Penzance, The Mikado, Iolanthe,* and *HMS Pinafore* with Sr. Suzanne directing the singing and Pat the acting.

Sr. Suzanne had her ways of persuading high school students to sing the parts. Catherine Regan, later a staff member at Mercy Center, remembers, "I was in *The Pirates of Penzance,* where I had to fill in. I didn't know if I could do it, but Suzanne had confidence in me. 'Oh, sure you can do it!' she told me breezily." Of course, Catherine did it and did it well.

"Pat became upset with the boys from Serra High School, who were supposed to be in the musicals, because they came late or not at all to rehearsals," said Sr. Suzanne. "She dismissed them, and we were to have no musical. One of the girls, Betsy O'Hearn, said that her father would love to be in the musicals. Thus started a wonderful tradition of having the girls' fathers play the male roles."

Some likely candidates tried to bow out.

Tim Regan, who lived nearby and later became Catherine's father-in-law, told Sr. Suzanne he couldn't be in the musical because he traveled. Suzanne settled it with, "You'll just have to be a pirate then." She apparently felt that pirates could travel, and she wouldn't take no for an answer.

"The men were faithful about the rehearsals and sang with more mature voices," said Sr. Suzanne. "They brought a note from their wives when they had to miss — their joke! A wonderful relationship developed between the girls and their fathers. And it was fun!

Sr. Suzanne continued to be successful with her choral groups, in fact too successful for some other chorale teachers. She may not have stressed classroom discipline, but musical discipline was at a high standard.

The Archdiocese of San Francisco set up an afternoon of music as a competition for chorales from girls' high schools. Sr. Suzanne trained her girls so well that the Burlingame chorale won year after year. There was some resentment about her success.

Sr. Pat, a loyal supporter, sat in the back of the auditorium one year when Sr. Suzanne brought a large glee club group and won. The chatter in the back was, "Well, if you bring the whole school!"

Stung by that criticism, Sr. Suzanne brought a small group the next year and won again. Pat heard the comment, "Well, if you bring only an elite group!"

Finally the archdiocese stopped the event. Apparently, no one could compete with her.

As a teacher, Sr. Suzanne gave the girls more than exposure to excellence; she enabled their own mystical experiences. She communicated the depth of her faith to them through singing and enlivened theirs. It was an experience of God for them, not just a performance.

"There is a unity of spirit in the singing," as she remembered with a note of longing in her voice. "I don't think there is anything comparable to it. With my high school chorus, there were moments you felt at-oneness. When they really experienced the music, they broke open the music and became part of it."

"I have never ever met anyone who conducted a choral group with that combination of wonderful technique and spirit," said Rey Friel, who was in the high school chorale and then in the community from 1963 to 1983. "We drilled and drilled, but when we went to perform, she said, 'Just forget everything you learned and sing with the Spirit.'

"She conducted with her whole body, not just her hands," said Rey reverently. "She danced the songs for us. She drew you in. The audience never saw her face and eyes. There was everything in them—quietness, happiness, sadness—almost like a mime."

At its best, the class was electric. She modeled and inspired her students with a music experience grounded in her faith. Hundreds of girls were moved and changed by her over her thirty years of teaching.

"It was important in my spirituality," said her former student Mary Gadson. "I didn't really understand the words of the prayers I said, but when I started to sing in chorale and listen to the words, it started to hit me. I started to understand what I was believing."

FOUR

The Power of Ritual

One could — as I have — define ritual as the opportunity to participate directly in a myth. It is the enactment of a mythical situation, and by participating in the rite, you participate in the myth.
                                        —Joseph Campbell, *Pathways to Bliss* *

♫ Mercy campus employees gathered at noontime in the darkened chapel. Each picked up a small smooth stone from a bowl at the entrance. Most fingered it with curiosity. They came because Sr. Suzanne's services often touched them, and it was Lent. Time for reconciliation.

The theme of the prayer and the readings was "Take from us our stony hearts and open us to the immensity of your mercy." The words described the hardness of our hearts, the heaviness of the burdens of wars, and starvation rampant in the world. Sr. Suzanne played the piano and sang with the group. Finally each was asked to come up and lay the stone in the basin on a cloth-covered altar, let go of its smoothness and the weight it represented. People came in a stream, unselfconscious and intent: the workers from the kitchen at ease only in Spanish, the accountant from the Philippines, administrative assistants, the Catholic housekeeping staff, the Sisters, and a lone Protestant.

---

*Joseph Campbell, *Pathways to Bliss* (Novato, CA: New World Library, 2004), 30.

73

Sr. Suzanne played through the ritual that she had written. Everything fit together into a whole each would remember: the simplicity of words; the small, cool stones; and the solemn walking forward with others.

After participating in Catholic ritual for thirty years, Sr. Suzanne began to experiment with prayer rituals after Vatican II. She has been asked to create "a little prayer service" hundreds of times each year. People want to focus on the planting of a memorial garden, the signing of an important document, or recognition of employees' service.

"There are special occasions," she wrote, "where the community assembles for prayer. Here the liturgist can be more free. The use of symbol and ritual is very important and can 'speak' what 'words' cannot."

What makes an effective ritual, whether we are speaking of the Eucharistic liturgy or a prayer service?

The word "ritual" evokes a range of associations from tea rituals, Indian rituals, and ritual dress to rituals of chocolate. The Internet yields thousands of references, suggesting we are a culture fascinated, even obsessed, with ritual. The pages of entries suggest that ritual pulls at something deep in us; covens and congregations try to enter those depths.

Mythologist Joseph Campbell defined ritual as myth enacted. "By participating in the rite, you participate in the myth." Myth marks a level of meaning and truth beyond that which can be proved scientifically or historically but which connects us to the transcendent God.

Campbell's meaning suggests that, as a culture, we may sometimes look for ritual in offbeat ways because we are looking for the connection to the ground of our being, to our very depths. We want to be taken out of our individual selves, sometimes because we are desperate for answers, sometimes because we seek pleasure, and often because we need community.

Our ordinary lives are riddled with what we call rituals on many levels. "Don't we have daily rituals — putting the right shoe on first, raising the blinds, and, next, looking for the coffee filters?" I asked Sr. Suzanne, thinking of how these movements seem like natural patterns.

Sr. Suzanne was quick to shake her head. "Those are only habits, repeated actions," she replied.

Reassuring, repetitive activities may frame our days, but they don't take us beyond ourselves into community or move us forward in our search for transcendence. They don't resonate with meaning; they help manage our physical existence. Habits are helpful on several levels. They keep us from having to decide how to do certain things each day: where to put the clean plates, for example, or when to brush our teeth. They save time and emotional stress. They may even help us become highly effective people.

What is ritual if it is not ritualized action? "True ritual is a matter of reaching deeper levels," said Sr. Suzanne. What is "beyond" calls us; we are searching for transcendence. How do we construct meaningful rituals as Christians?

Christian ritual differs sharply from natural, secular ritual, which also can illuminate meaning. The ceremony of joining the Girl Scouts is a familiar secular ritual. Standing in a circle, giving the Girl Scout promise, getting the green sash and the badges signifies belonging to a group of peers who agree to a code of behavior (strive to build a campfire properly, safely take care of toddlers, and generally become a responsible eight-year-old).

Becoming a Girl Scout might be important, but the pinning ceremony doesn't make a statement about the connection of the eight-year-old to the universe.

The impulse to create ritual is strong. Watch children bury a dead bird or pet turtle. Even though they may never have been to a funeral, they often make a simple ceremony to express their feelings of solemnity: wrapping the body, carefully filling in the dirt, placing a marker, and saying a few words. I remember a group of us, all about age six, stuffing a dead turtle in a Band-Aid box and burying him with sad words in the backyard — childish, of course, but how like what we do as adults. We like to mark certain events as special, make them stand out in the flow of time.

The ceremony of stones Sr. Suzanne created for Lent went beyond the basics of the turtle burial and even the Girl Scout ceremony. Her words and music connected people to their faith and to each other.

She likes examples from our secular life to illustrate her discussions of ritual. "Football games are rituals," said Sr. Suzanne, although she confesses she has been to only one or two. "There's the gathering of people, the focus on the action, food, vocalizations, gestures — that is secular ritual. It must do something for people! I can see that there is a feeling of camaraderie from it."

She's more familiar with birthday parties. (Even nuns celebrate birthdays occasionally, although feast days are more important.)

"A birthday party is a kind of ritual." She listed its characteristics:

- People gather for a purpose.

- A leader gets people's attention and does the presentation.

- There are symbols used (cake, candles).

- People tell stories (sometimes recounting the birth of the child),

- There is song.

- There is gesture or action (presentation of the cake and blowing out of candles).

- There is a sort of meal (people eat the cake).

These "birthday party" elements of ritual are the bones of a liturgy, the underlying structure. All liturgies are filled with ritual, but not all rituals are liturgies. Some rituals are simple but important ceremonies: the blessing of a house, the beginning of a gathering, the investiture of a leader.

In creating rituals that express our faith, we make certain distinctions. Christian ritual is not magic; it is not propitiation of a god. Prayers and blessings are not spells. The ritual of baptism doesn't change the nature of a child from evil to saved; it is symbolic of an interior event and of the inclusion of a child in the community.

The liturgy of the Mass is essentially a "birthday party," since Christ is made present in the gathering with the help of all these elements of ritual. Together they give us a sense of completeness, a sense of participation in Christ's community. "In Christian terms the life, death, and resurrection of Jesus is the sacred story," said Sr. Suzanne. "We want to get in touch, to access that sacred story central to our belief. We access it through ritual. We come to something within ourselves that is very present to the reality. It transcends what is right here. A ritual allows the person to enter the transcendent reality.

"To be effective, the liturgist needs to help the assembly to come to the ritual, to use signs and symbols that are transparent, that help to gather the energy of the group and the individuals," said Sr. Suzanne. "How the gathering is done is important. There needs to be a conscious sense of gathering and welcome in the entrance song and procession. The priest is there to gather the prayers of the people and offer them, not to perform or to conduct a public meeting."

Sr. Suzanne has been attuned to the wise directive of the bishops' committee on liturgy in 1972 that liturgical signs "must be simple and comprehensible."

"The liturgy is full of symbols: the table facing the people, the cross, candles, bread and wine, the vestments, the Scriptures. The liturgist can 'muck it up' by using symbols that are complicated or get in the way; he can indulge in over-explanation." She was perhaps thinking of the post-Vatican II commentator who seemed to her to obscure the liturgical experience rather than clarify it.

"Unless a symbol can speak for itself, it is not doing its job. If the liturgist or pastor has to talk about what it means, it isn't effective," Sr. Suzanne continued.

"The stories are the Scriptures read clearly. The prayers are for specific people and causes. Rich ritual gestures run through the entire liturgy: the carrying of the Scriptures in the procession, the priest opening his hands in welcome to pray, his hands over the elements, genuflection, the kiss of peace, people crossing themselves in blessing. The meal and the music feed body and soul."

Ritual for Sr. Suzanne is about inclusion of all present. The gesture, symbols, and patterns come together for a satisfying event when they are expressive of belief. They are not magic acts that operate without the participants. When belief structures change, rituals must change, as can be illustrated by changes in religious life.

Throughout the history of its community, the Sisters of Mercy have had a number of structures that resonated with meaning. The goal of the horarium (the daily schedule of the community) was to point toward God through prayer on an hourly or at least regular basis.

"We did have patterns in religious life that we have changed," Sr. Suzanne said. "When I entered, as we passed each other in the hallway, the senior sister would say routinely, 'Praise be to Jesus Christ,' and the other would reply, 'and to His Blessed Mother.' We got up every weekday morning at 5:00 a.m. and were meditating in the chapel at 5:25 a.m. Some of us found it very difficult to stay awake then. But you could go about your day without thinking about what you would do next, so you could think about God. Ideally the structure would lead to silence.

"As things changed, these patterns became only ritualized actions, not rituals leading to God. We got rid of these things [the hourly structure, the formalized and hierarchical greetings]. Although they were set up to be helpful originally, they lost their sense and we got rid of them."

The Sisters let go of their monastic routines and enjoyed more flexibility and freedom in their prayer lives. In the Mass, the priest now faces the assembly at the altar, not the sanctuary cross. The symbolic action is inclusive of the people, not a gesture of the priest alone reaching up to God. Liturgists emphasize changes such as silence after the readings because they point to our renewed understanding of the importance of the Word.

Another example of what seemed to me to be a flawed ritual came from a funeral Sr. Suzanne and I discussed. The Protestant pastor had met the deceased ninety-year-old woman only a few times and opened the service with some general, casual remarks about her, acknowledging the family and their grief. He then invited others to come up to the podium. A few did, one or two with off the cuff stories and one with notes. Most of the friends of the dear woman were quite elderly and lacked the stamina to talk about her.

The pastor then moved into a few prayers, ending with the Lord's Prayer. There was no form, traditional or newly created, no elevated language, no music, few actions or gestures and nothing to move the congregation beyond this moment. I missed the sense of a container, some ritual worthy of recognizing this moment in the life of a mother, wife, and grandmother.

When not enough of the bones of ritual as solemn container show through, a service can feel made up of disconnected, random elements. There is no recognizable pattern, ritualized or otherwise.

Sr. Suzanne talked about a ritual she had created that felt inadequate to her. She had led the group of women in a ceremony of exchanging candles during morning chapel, and she felt it wasn't a success. In talking about it, she shook her head and fumed quietly, her brow furrowed, her voice trailing off into inner space.

"To have kept it in silence would have brought it deeper," she said.

Sometimes no explanation is needed. The ritual penetrates the heart. At the end of the funerals of Mercy Sisters the entire community would stand outside the Motherhouse chapel, lining the long drive in farewell as the hearse left for the cemetery. It was a simple, but powerful ritual. Our belief in God's promises should make that sad gesture of good-bye unnecessary, but as Keith Pecklers says in *Worship,* "Ritual is intimately linked with the body."* True elements of ritual leave us feeling satisfied, filled, and connected to each other and to the Holy. If we were only spirit, we wouldn't need ritual. Ritual is rooted in being human.

---

*Keith Pecklers, *Worship: A Primer in Christian Ritual* (Minneapolis: Augsburg Fortress Press, 1997), 6.

"Christ was the most human of all beings," said Sr. Suzanne in giving a Lenten day of prayer. "He was loving, full of integrity, justice, and peace. Holiness is a matter of becoming more human."

Christ came in a body. We need to recognize our bodies when we act out our faith — kneeling, standing, sitting, bowing — entering into the experience with others. Rituals can help us become more human, not abstracted versions of ourselves.

An effective ritual helps participants connect with God's immanence in community and with God's transcendence. The pattern of movement, symbol, and word shines like a jewel laid into the everyday — the ordinary made sacred.

◆ ◆ ◆

Sr. Suzanne offers guiding questions for any ritual:

- Is the purpose of the service clear?
- Do the symbols you have chosen speak to the people present?
- Is there a pattern and a unity to the service?
- Are the words eloquent?
- Do the actions and gestures express what people believe?

THE FOCUS OF LITURGY

When we become aware of the God who *is* — imaged in people, in nature, in the beautiful movement of the universe — we feel impelled to acknowledge God. As we begin to know God, we are intrigued. Then we begin to entrust our lives to God. We begin to attune our lives, and our values change. As we become more God centered, we begin to see ourselves and all creation as one in God.

Liturgy helps us do this, not just individually but also communally because we are social beings. We worship together, not just through prayer but by ritual action. Ritual expresses who we are in a bodily way, using words, gestures, story, and song, all of which involve the heart.

For Catholics, Eucharist is the ritual that is the source and summit of our life in Christ: source because in it we are deeply united with Christ; summit because it is the pinnacle of life in Christ. It is Christ's action of self-giving; Christ embraces all that is human and offers it to the Source (Father). We unite ourselves to this giving.

The goal of liturgy is to enable all of us to come to Eucharist just as we are. We are welcomed with our life just as it is, with all our hope and dreams, our troubles with work or family. We come with what hurts us and what makes us happy, with our failings and successes, with the totality of our humanness. We come to Eucharist to be joined in the movement of the Spirit to Christ's great act of self-giving.

The elements of liturgy — the music, the environment, the readers, the presider, the homily — all have this one great focus. This is a place where we hope to have little ego. We all want to bring ourselves to Eucharist. It is something we never do wholeheartedly, but we keep trying.

As musicians we want to be the best that we can; we want to know and love our craft, but as Brother Roger of Taizé once said of liturgical music, it must be like John the Baptist, always pointing to Christ and never to itself.

FIVE

Articulating Belief
through Music

We look at how well this piece of music expresses the faith of Church in this time and place and expresses the mystery of God. How well does it enable the assembly to give voice to their hope?"
— Diana Macalintal, Director of Worship,
Diocese of San Jose, California

♫ Kids and adults are gathered around the campfire, all belting out the words to "She'll Be Coming Round the Mountain," which gives way to "Good Night, Sweetheart," and at the very end, as the fire flickers down, "Kumbaya."

Kumbaya, my Lord, kumbaya
Someone's singing, Lord, kumbaya

That evening is deeply imbedded in my memory: singing the songs, eating burnt marshmallows, and snuggling deeper into my sweatshirt. Community is not so much articulated as acted out. The heartfelt singing is a kind of ceremony, quieting, healing the pain of the day or uniting people in a purpose. How does this differ from a liturgical moment?

Listening to Sr. Suzanne's outgoing voicemail gives a clue. "I am on the tel-e-phone." A clearly articulated message with a hint of melody in her voice. Years of practicing diction with choruses and congregations are imprinted on each word.

Sr. Suzanne was exact with her high school students. As a choral director standing in front of the girls, she demonstrated how to open their mouths fully three fingers high, to sing out, remembered Mercy High alumna Mary Williamson Gadson. "Sing from the diaphragm," Sr. Suzanne would say. "I want to hear to the last 't,' don't let it just drop off. People need to understand you," she insisted.

"In a lot of church songs, you don't understand the words," said Mary, "but she wanted you to understand the words, especially in her music. She wanted people to hear what she had to say."

"Kumbaya" is a fine song, apparently from the Gullah people living in the Sea Islands off the coast of Georgia and South Carolina, but its original meanings for my generation have faded off into good intentions. It symbolizes things we fumbled toward, especially in the 1960s and 1970s — unity, change, justice for all. One of the strengths of the song is that a spectrum of people with a variety of beliefs and goals can come together under the generous umbrella of its words.

As a composer, Sr. Suzanne has always been particular about the meanings of her lyrics, not just the melody of her tunes. She understood what the bishops were trying to do with the bishops' Committee on the Liturgy. She was one of the organizers of Mercy liturgical conferences in the 1950s. The Mercy nuns were eager to find out what the latest was on liturgy.

Sr. Suzanne was instrumental in having a dialogue Mass at the Motherhouse whenever they could find a priest who would allow them to participate by saying the responses. Owning the words at least by saying them, even in Latin, was an important step.

In many liturgies, hymns are just a change of pace from the reading of the Scripture and the prayers of the faithful. But they can be among the most powerful words in the liturgy. Composer Fr. John Olivier, SS, music director for St. Patrick's Seminary in Menlo Park, articulated what keeps composers conscious of text: "Church music is a great vehicle of faith. We remember phrases and hymns for a long time."

As Fr. Olivier implied, expressive songs require more than a steady, rousing beat with a singable melody. They require words with carefully chosen meanings.

The point was made clear to Sr. Suzanne during the summer of 1953. As a young nun, she was taking a class in requiems from the acclaimed choral director Robert Shaw at San Diego State College. For the curriculum, the students sang great religious works by Bach, Berlioz, Fauré, and Brittan.

"I was the only nun in the class and in a full habit," she said. "It was a great summer of singing with a choir. Every class before we sang, Shaw would do an exegesis of the text of all these great works, and I saw and felt how important text is. A key moment for me was when I heard the closing chorale chorus of Bach's *Passion of St. John.** It was my first experience of being part of the Passion and it made a glorious impression on me that has lasted through my life:

> *Lord Jesus, thy dear angels send*
> *When e'er my mortal life shall end,*
> *And bear my soul to heaven.*
> *Within its narrow chamber keep*
> *My body safe in painless sleep*
> *Till thy last call be given.*
>
> *And when from death thou wakest me,*
> *In bliss untold mine eyes shall see,*

---

*The official title of this work is *The Passion of Our Lord Jesus Christ According to St. John.*

O Son of God, thy glorious face,
My savior and my font of grace.
Lord Jesus Christ, O hear thou me,
O hear thou me,
*Thee will I praise eternally.**

Transfixed by the soaring glory of both music and words, Sr. Suzanne carried that moment with her into teaching choral works to high school students and younger novices. Her choral class was more effective than a religion class in inspiring the girls because Sr. Suzanne radiated love for the music. They sang Randall Thompson's "Alleluia," Vittoria's "O Magnum Mysterium," and works by Palestrina. They sang Bach.

Forty years later, students and novices look to their Toolan choral experience as the source and guide for their current spirituality. "She probably had one of the biggest influences on my spirituality," said Lorraine Paul, who was in the Mercy convent from 1968 to 1972. "Through song she expressed her faith, her joy for life, her belief in God."

Because she is acutely aware that hymns articulate belief, Sr. Suzanne has standards for excellence in the texts that balance poetry, rhythm, and sound theology. She is critical of sentimental songs and sappy words. She shudders at texts such as "Little King So Fair and Sweet." Dreamy idealism and cloying words are part of what makes a "shabby composer."

But what should we sing? Her distaste signals one of her criteria. Sentimentality is a kind of emotional trickery practiced by Victorian hymn writers. Their sticky nineteenth century quality is not just bad art; it lacks authenticity for today's congregations. Text is powerful when the people

---

*Closing chorale of *The Passion According to St. John,* English translation and adaptation by Rev. J. Troutbeck, D.D. (London: Novello & Co.).

mean what they sing. She took pains to make sure her students understood what they were singing. It became part of them and encouraged their faith.

When Vatican II's Constitution on the Sacred Liturgy directed that the liturgy be in the vernacular, Sr. Suzanne was ready. What better source for sound theology than Scripture? For words, she went to a favorite source, the Gospel of John, and the music came:

> *I am the Bread of life.*
> *You who come to me shall not hunger.*
> *You who believe in me shall not thirst.*
> *No one can come to me*
> *Unless the Father draw you.**

John's words express spiritual desires in words of simple human experiences — thirst and hunger. Set to her tune, they provide deeply felt hope. They pull singers together in a sense of community with Christ. Sr. Suzanne said, "People have told me that putting the Eucharist and resurrection together is what makes it powerful. I did that because I was writing for a Eucharistic event for the archdiocese."

Liturgical music commentator Dr. Fred Molek observed that part of what makes "I Am the Bread of Life" so convincing is that "when we sing that octave leap in the refrain, the prophecy is sounded of being raised up, and we even know when — on the last day." The music and words work perfectly together.

Using Scripture as text seems logical forty-five years later, but at the time, musicians and liturgists were groping. Suddenly, congregations were expected to participate in the

---

*"I Am the Bread," GIA copyright © 2003.

service by responding, praying, and singing in English. The problem was complex.

Words had to be expressive of belief, but singing the Baltimore Catechism wouldn't do it.

Songs needed to be inspirational, lyrical, and easy for people to learn. The folk Mass was only a gleam in the eyes of the St. Louis Jesuits.

"I Am the Bread of Life" became wildly popular. The National Association of Pastoral Musicians founder Fr. Virgil Funk calls it "the most significant piece of music before Michael Joncas. It became the most sung piece of music of the time."

The words articulate faith in a directly understandable way. They draw on Jesus' promises to his people recorded in Scripture. Unlike "Kumbaya," they express more than good feeling; they express hope woven into the larger fabric of belief.

Sr. Suzanne's familiarity with Scripture helps her, but she admitted to other resources. "I go to the Bible and take down the text that I like. Then I try to think of other related texts. I have to say, I've even used the concordance." For the "Friendship Hymn" she drew on John and Sirach; for the "Hymn of Joy" she used words from John, Paul, and Ezekiel.

She told of a backhanded compliment from a student at Mercy High School years ago. "I wrote so much using the words of John's Gospel that one day a student came to me after Mass. She said, 'They used your words in Church today.'" Sr. Suzanne laughed at the memory, but in a sense the words of the Gospel have become her words, intimately known and deeply understood.

Hymn writing is an art of stitching words together, not just sticking them in place. They are artfully and carefully chosen. Using a concordance, a different translation, or phrases from different passages all make the words work. She has a few guidelines for choosing texts.

First, text needs to reflect the experience of a community as directly and powerfully as possible. Emotion belongs here. "One does not have to have a lecture on St. Ignatius," Sr. Suzanne told pastoral musicians several years ago, "to grasp what the psalmist is saying when he writes, 'My whole being thirsts for God, the living God; how long till I come and see the face of God.' That is a universal cry of restlessness that each one of us has experienced." Helping a congregation express loss and pain directly is a ministry. She points to Brian Wren's words as particularly powerful. His "When Grief Is Raw" to a tune by David Haas is a meaningful choice for a funeral:

> *When grief is raw*
> *and music goes unheard*
> *and thought is numb,*
> *we have no polished phrases to recite.*
> *In Christ we come*
> *to hear the old familiar words:*
> *"I am the resurrection. I am the life."**

Second, the words should reflect what we believe, or aspire to believe, or we are only mouthing syllables. Words should be treated as respectfully as dynamite. Sr. Suzanne has changed her own theology and wants her words to change as well. Over the last twenty-five years she became aware that the concept of God she reflected in her texts was too narrow. She could no longer think of God as only masculine. "To name God either he or she, man or woman limits God who is beyond all naming, certainly beyond our limitations in

---

*"When Grief Is Raw," GIA copyright © 2003.

gender," she said. God is not "he" in prayers and creeds at the Motherhouse chapel. God is simply God.

She has made changes in her old texts, replacing he referring to God or to the believer with whatever will work. "I Am the Bread" originally said "He who comes to Me shall not hunger." Now the lines say, "You who come to Me." She acknowledges that changes are sometimes difficult, but choices can be made. Words are too powerful to be ignored. She is adamant that mixed congregations not sing "Good Christian Men Rejoice!" for example.

She doesn't shy away from giving opinions about war when she feels it is urgent.

> *Let us lay down our weapons of might.*
> *Stockpiles but lead to terror and fright.*
> *Wealth that is wasted, anger unfurled.*
> *Let bombs be changed to bread for the world.*
> *Let us walk in justice,*
> *Let us walk in mercy,*
> *Let us walk humbly with our God.* *

As Sr. Suzanne's careful selections show, finding a hymn text that "suits us" is like finding a bloom of words that brings to fullness what is in us. The words may bring reassurance, or they can simply move us a step further toward clarity.

God certainly doesn't require us to be articulate. The benefit is obviously on our side. Feeling emerges into the light of expression, even if it is an upwelling of pain as in Job's cry, "I will speak in the anguish of my spirit" (Job 7:11, RSV).

When we sing the traditional gems, the thoughts and faith of those who came before are carried in the words; they are shaped from use like stones polished in a river. We feel their

*"Let Us Walk in Justice," © 2005, Suzanne Toolan. Published by OCP Publications, 5536 NE Hassalo, Portland, OR 07213. All rights reserved. Used with permission.

power, yet sometimes their shape becomes unrecognizable, and we need to begin with new words. That struggle to reflect our beliefs more truly drove the liturgical movement in the twentieth century, emerging in the reforms of Vatican II.

Diana Macalintal, director of worship for the Diocese of San Jose, California, reinforces Sr. Suzanne's sense that message is central to music chosen. "I see a maturity in the Church today in its understanding of music. When we work at our best, the Church and its musicians don't look at a particular style or date of writing [of a piece], or whether it is in Latin or not. We look at how well this piece of music expresses the faith of Church in this time and place and [how well it] expresses the mystery of God. How well does it enable the assembly to give voice to their hope?"

As Sr. Suzanne said in 1980 in a talk to pastoral musicians, entitled "Mean What You Sing": "Music has the special way of letting us linger over the words. It has a special way of touching our hearts, of laying open the mystery. Because it is a social art it enables us to do this together as a community. Music enlarges and expands the message. We join one another in enthusiasm for the message. A good song does not preach; it sometimes interprets Scripture. It plants a message in our hearts, a message to be mulled over to become part of us."

The sweeping melodic lines of her "Ephesians Hymn" bring the words alive:

> *May Christ live in your heart.*
> *Through faith may he be with you.*
> *That rooted and built in love*
> *You may proclaim his goodness.*
> *If you live by truth and love in the Lord Jesus,*
> *God's great gift will be proclaimed in you."**

---

*"Ephesians Hymn II," GIA copyright © 1966.

Shaping the Bread of Life

*Mother Church earnestly desires that all the faithful should
be led to that full conscious and active participation in liturgical celebrations which is demanded by the very nature of
the liturgy.* —Constitution on the Sacred Liturgy, II, 14

Sr. Suzanne rushed up the hill from the convent to her
music room in the rose-brick high school building. Although
she was doing what she loved, time was always scarce. She was
teaching music and religion, conducting chorale, composing, and
directing Gilbert and Sullivan productions at the high school. As
she often did, she was playing with sounds in her head and was
eager to sit down at the piano. She had in mind a favorite text from
the Gospel of John 6:35: "I am the bread of life."

It was January 1966 and the routine of morning prayers, Mass,
and breakfast was behind her. She had quickly put on her long
black habit with the long sleeves, the veil over the white coif and
the heavy rosary around her waist, though how she exactly looked
she couldn't be sure. No mirrors were allowed in the convent. She
could catch a glimpse of her tall figure in a window reflection if she
were quick, but she wasn't that interested.

An archdiocesan event, a meeting of the National Catholic Music
Educators in San Francisco, was looming, and she had been asked
to write the communion hymn for it. As usual, she had put off writing, although music seemed to flow out of her fingers. The more
that was demanded of her, the more she produced.

"I love to compose for a group that I know for an occasion," she said. "I find it hard to sit down and compose without a goal." Deadlines fed her creativity, but she was famous for procrastination and for accepting extra work. She had begun the practice of writing a piece for each high school graduating class to be performed by her chorale. "Thou Art Fair" in 1954 was the first. The girls were delighted by the attention and took special pride in "their" song.

Sr. Suzanne loved sounds of trained women's voices — the lifts, the crisp endings, and especially the thick harmonies — each vocal line woven into a fabric. Her high school students in their plaid uniforms rehearsed in the old Kohl Mansion's Great Hall, and although Suzanne insisted that discipline was not her strong point, she had only to rap on her music stand, and the girls would straighten up and sing.

Sr. Suzanne had created the schola, the group of novices she rehearsed to sing at Masses and other ceremonies. The schola nuns were chosen by her personal invitation, but the whole Mercy community, responding to her encouragement, delighted in singing harmony, often breaking out into song on a bus trip or during a community meeting.

"I remember Bishop Pierre DuMaine asking if it were requisite that girls coming into the community be able to sing in four parts," said Sr. Suzanne, "because the whole community (with a few tone-deaf exceptions) sang in four-part harmony."

Her work had begun to take a new direction with a public event in 1964. The Sisters of Mercy in Burlingame were responding to the concern of Pope Pius XII that religious in the United States go to assist the Latin American Church. At this point "assist" meant that they were missionaries in countries where the Church was at risk.

Pictures show Sr. Mary Cyril Driscoll, Superior General, in full habit, signing documents that sent four Mercys into the harsh conditions of the cold, 12,000-foot-high Altiplano of Peru. Many Sisters of Mercy from Burlingame volunteered, but only four were chosen at first, although ultimately fourteen worked in the impoverished Altiplano with the poorest of the poor.

Her superior had asked her to write a piece to celebrate their departure. Sr. Suzanne, as usual, procrastinated until perilously close to the ceremony. At dinner, General Council member Sr. Mary Marcella said impatiently to her, "Well, I see you won't have the piece done and the program has to be printed. We'll just have to sing something else."

Sr. Suzanne remembers that, stung into action, still in her blue kitchen apron, she flounced all the way to her music room at the high school, her habit swaying, and, fueled by indignation, finished off "The Mission Hymn." The result was a rousing and triumphant tune, fitting for the Sisters going with the idea of converting those in primitive lands. The hymn was sung at the ceremony at Our Lady of Angels Church, a parish near the Motherhouse. The words from Isaiah convey the idea:

> *Great is the Lord, worthy of praise*
> *Tell all the nations God is King!*
> *Spread the news of his love!*
> *The Spirit of the Lord is upon me*
> *because the Lord has anointed me.*
> *He has sent me to bring glad tidings*
> *to the lowly, to the lowly.**

The high-ceilinged church was bursting with excited nuns and families, and the Sisters were appropriately sent off into the unknown with a strong expression of love and faith. A photo shows four of them the next day in full black habit, smiling, about to board their plane. The Mercy community, including Sr. Suzanne, was happy to be able to respond to the Pope's request.

---

*"The Mission Hymn," GIA copyright © 1966.

Sr. Suzanne had no interest in flying off to a foreign country herself. The idea made her shudder. She delighted in conducting chorale and the schola. She felt her place was clearly at home.

Over the next few years, the Sisters who went to Peru to teach doctrine realized the deep spirituality of the Aymara people which had blended with their Catholicism. Their mission changed to one of "walking with" the people, being attentive to their healing practices and encouraging their sense of self-worth, especially among the women.

"The Mission Hymn" attracted attention for its singable, clean lines and its vigorous tune. It gave Sr. Suzanne her first taste of fame. Sr. Mary Assumpta Murray, who went to Peru in 1962 to scout out the location and who was known for her solid judgment and excellent memory into her nineties, admired the "The Mission Hymn" as Sr. Suzanne's best piece.

"I can see the good-bye here," remembered the late Sr. Mary Assumpta forty-two years later, "as the Sisters sang out in front of the Motherhouse before the four went to the airport. That's my first recollection of an outstanding hymn she wrote. That is the 'big one' for me."

The departure of the four highlights a key aspect of Suzanne's life: she never lived anywhere but on the Burlingame campus, an unusual fact for Sisters, who were moved frequently and often against their wishes. She was never uprooted to teach music at another of the Mercy schools throughout California although she did commute to the nearby Mercy High San Francisco and to St. Patrick's Seminary to teach the seminarians. The reasons are unclear and probably buried with the former superiors, but she settled into the campus and it became part of her, the dark wood and high windows of her beloved chapel, the wide convent halls, the lushness of the lawns and lower meadow. She wasn't limited by staying in one place; the stability fed her, and the beauty of the forty acres influenced her music.

On this particular chilly day two years after the Peru departure, Sr. Suzanne wanted to make sure of what her chorale classes would be singing. Always walking around with notes in her head, she was mulling over text as well, and she wanted to find a time during the day to work on the music.

As a musician, Sr. Suzanne was cheered by what had happened two years before at Vatican II, signaling changes, not just in the music but also in the Church's attitude toward liturgical celebrations. As a liturgist, she had her own sense of direction. Almost from her first vows in 1952, she had introduced singing during daily Mass at the convent because to her worship was inconceivable without it.

"Our ceremony music was in Latin, for receiving Sisters into the community for instance," she remembered. "I did one ceremony in English translated from Latin by Sr. Ellen FitzGerald, and I got into trouble. Superior Mother Cyril angrily called me into her office and said, 'Even I would not have done this!' She made such a fuss. You had to get permission from the archbishop, which of course I didn't have. But when Mother Cyril heard the novices loved it, she allowed us to do it."

But music was a problem for Catholics, Sr. Suzanne thought, partly because they were so used to just listening. Although her experience with Protestants was limited in these early years, she admired them. She was later to work with many Protestant groups in ecumenical concerts and at Mercy Center. "In the movies, anyway, the Protestants sing," she said earnestly.

This musician's irritation with "sappy things" or "schmaltz" was well-known even in her early teaching career. Her classical music training tuned her instincts for what was well written and unsentimental. Fr. John Olivier, composer and conductor at nearby St. Patrick's Seminary, was one of the first outside the community to discover Sr. Suzanne's talents. Watching her conduct her Sisters and listening to her music in the 1960s, he was reverential. "We had someone here who was delicately sensitive to Scripture and prayer, a fine musician," he said.

Sr. Suzanne had only tolerated the *St. Gregory Hymnal,* which was used throughout the English-speaking Catholic Church from 1920s to the 1960s. She wrinkled her nose at "Jesus Thou Art Coming," and "Little King So Fair and Sweet." The combination of the theology of Jesus as a meek, sugary figure with what she regarded as badly written music was too much for her.

Sr. Suzanne reacted negatively to "bad art" in worship because she felt it obscured the worship experience. How can people best experience community and the presence of God? Her answer was in accord with the liturgical changes of Vatican II even before the bishops expressed them. The Constitution on the Sacred Liturgy addressed the broader core issue, the people's relationship to the liturgy:

> *Mother Church earnestly desires that all the faithful should be led to that full conscious and active participation in liturgical celebrations which is demanded by the very nature of the liturgy.*   —Constitution on the Sacred Liturgy, II, 14

This winter day sitting at the high school piano in 1966 she would compose a hymn that would not be her first work in English. She was in the habit of writing a piece for each graduating class, which they treasured, but they were written in four-part harmony for experienced voices. She wanted a piece that people could sing in church, unrehearsed, in English.

She was about to compose a piece which would further the active participation of the people. At a break in her chorale classes, she took refuge in the music room in the Kohl Mansion, which houses part of the high school. The room next to it served as an infirmary where students sometimes enjoyed a little rest in the name of recuperating from a headache. Relatively undisturbed in this room off the Great Hall, she sat at the school piano and worked out a melody for a new hymn.

The words "I am the Bread of life, he who comes to me shall not hunger" seemed to fit naturally into notes.

> *I am the Bread of life.*
> *He who comes to me shall not hunger;*
> *He who believes in me shall not thirst.*
> *No one can come to me unless the Father draw him.*
> *And I will raise him up on the last day.* *

At this time she didn't worry about the implications of non-inclusive language. Later, her consciousness raised, she changed the words to "And I will raise them up," or at the funeral of a woman, "I will raise her up."

But the piece didn't seem right to her.

"I was frustrated with it and threw it in the trash," Sr. Suzanne said of her now famous work. Her sense of inadequacy as a composer made her doubt her work, as was frequently the case. Fortunately a student lying on a bed in the infirmary next door spoke up, "What was that? It was beautiful!"

Sr. Suzanne got the piece of paper out of the trash and taped it together. The piece premiered at the National Catholic Music Educators' Association convention in San Francisco that March.

Today she can't quite bring herself to understand the success of the hymn. "'I Am the Bread of Life' is popular because it was the beginning of using Scripture as text," she admitted. "It had a chorus people liked, but it shouldn't really work. It's not metric. It is difficult to sing. It goes too high and too low. Someone I know gave talks on how it should not work. But people like a recurring thing—'I will raise you up.' I don't know," she trailed off, not quite willing to accept the vitality of the piece.

---

*"I Am the Bread of Life," GIA copyright © 1966.

After she had distributed it for free on her own for a while, the Archdiocese of San Francisco recommended her music to GIA, and Robert Batastini, its editor, took it. "There is probably not one single parish in the USA (and many elsewhere) that has not sung this hymn," said Bob. "It has been translated into a number of other languages, and appears in a number of Protestant hymnals as well."

Looking back, Fr. Roc O'Connor, SJ, one of the St. Louis Jesuits, saw that the Church was attempting to expand the horizontal action of the liturgy — the sense of community prayer. The vertical movement of the individual to God had been predominant; the sense of the transcendent in the Mass, the reality of the unchanging Holy, was there even if people in the congregation didn't participate with one another. Quick Masses in Latin didn't destroy the core of meaning, but Vatican II signaled a shift of effort. The new music of the time began to bring people together.

"In the early 1970s, the question was how we explore and involve people in communal singing. In our earliest writings, it was about integration of the two, the vertical and the horizontal aspects of the liturgy," said Fr. Roc.

The Church in general was groping for music in the vernacular. The obvious idea was to write music using Scripture for text, but the obvious hadn't come clear to composers. Sr. Suzanne knew text was extremely important. The choral director Robert Shaw had showed her the way years before during a summer choral class she had taken in San Diego.

Sr. Suzanne's work was an important part of moving church music from the mysterious and comforting dark of Latin into the light of the vernacular. Congregations were invited to move from the role of audience to that of community.

Fr. Virgil Funk, founder and president emeritus of the National Association of Pastoral Musicians, looks to Sr. Suzanne for her profound influence on Catholics singing in church. "With 'I Am the

Bread of Life,'" congregations knew that the text they were singing had meaning," he said forty years later. "Her song was one of the first that made that clear to everyone."

Congregations have loved it all over the globe and sing it with enthusiasm and heart. The hope of resurrection expressed in the text "I will raise you up" infuses people with hope. They sing the lines in French, in Spanish, in German, in accented English. The hymn has truly become bread for the world.

SIX

Creating Authentic Celebrations

Manifest plainness,
Embrace simplicity,
Reduce selfishness,
Have few desires.

—Lao-tzu (604–531 BC)
The Way of Lao-tzu

'Tis a gift to be simple, 'tis a gift to be free,
'Tis a gift to come down where we ought to be,
And when we find ourselves in the place just right,
'Twill be in the valley of love and delight.

—Shaker Elder Joseph Brackett, Jr. (1848)

♫ The Mercy Motherhouse vestry held an odd assortment of objects waiting to decorate the chapel: yards of gauzy gold cloth, stacks of tea lights, and a small candelabra. A diminutive granite angel guarded anointing oils and among small painted crosses that stuck up here and there.

"This is gimmicky stuff," Sr. Suzanne said frowning and lowering her voice conspiratorially. For someone who rarely shows disapproval, she might as well have been shouting. She had led me into the vestry that afternoon to show objects brought by a visiting group for services in the chapel. She shivered slightly.

"Sometimes things are gimmicks because they are too obvious and trite," she explained back in the cool order of her office. "A lot of the things we saw there in the vestry are

102

gimmicks because they are simply meant to catch people's attention. They have no depth to them."

What makes depth? I wondered. What about the great cathedrals of Europe with statues of saints in every corner, overfed cherubs, votive lights in their colored cups? Are they gimmicky?

And was Sr. Suzanne overlooking a quality for liturgy necessary for a modern congregation fed on digital sound and image bites? Isn't good liturgy a form of well-scripted entertainment, choreographed movements, attractive costumes, and appropriate props?

People in the Middle Ages needed pictures and statues in part because they didn't read. They needed visual help to tell the stories. The Renaissance overflowed with the exuberance of the senses in churches and cathedrals. Incense, banners, God on the ceiling in gorgeous robes, statues to touch in every nook.

Are all these parts of the experience of liturgy just gimmicks? Tricks encrusted with age and tradition to capture our attention? Consider that perhaps we need them in our humanness. Maybe granite angels have their place. If we are to capture people's attention, maybe we need more effects, not fewer. Most church services must be the most low-tech experience of the week for people who are surrounded by high-definition television and iPods.

Sr. Suzanne has led many Triduum services, which have a quality of carefully crafted drama. White-robed readers take their places on Good Friday, proclaiming Jesus' path toward the cross that day. The assembly chants a response at appropriate moments in the reading. The music is understated and meditative.

To attend Triduum closely is to enter the story. On Good Friday, a concentrated hush sifts down into the pews even as the kneelers creak with comings and goings. The congregation is immersed, drawn in by the empty tabernacle and the wood of the cross. We imagine Jesus stumbling. We hear Pontius Pilate ask, "What is truth?"

The Lutheran theologian Frank C. Senn suggests liturgy is enchantment in its deepest sense. "Enchantment casts a spell that leads one from a drab world to a brighter, more interesting world," he wrote.* Senn makes the point that mere entertainment makes us feel satisfied but doesn't move us to another level. On the other hand, he sees enchantment as taking us into a world that, in focusing on Spirit and story, asks us to change. Serious drama can affect us deeply. *Oedipus Rex* and *Death of a Salesman* reveal truths that have become deeply imprinted on our culture and that we can ponder throughout our lives. But liturgy enchants us as it draws us into the story of faith, the retelling of the truths we believe as a Christian community, moving us toward transformation, not merely satisfaction. Sr. Suzanne intuitively strives for this enchantment, a pure state of focus, in the liturgies. How that is achieved is the question. The materials of the creation of enchantment are the issue. Tea lights? Lots of small crosses on an altar? What is distracting "stuff," as she would say? What is essential for liturgy?

For her, environment creates or distracts from liturgical enchantment. The altar flowers, the shape of the tabernacle, the movements of the participants all are essential elements.

She has practiced what liturgical consultants help parishes to think about: a careful selection of the art and architecture of the worship space. Grace is offered by the surroundings, or not. Although some large suburban churches have every facility for light and sound shows available in the early

---

*Frank Senn, *Christian Liturgy* (Minneapolis: Augsburg Fortress, 1997), 704.

twenty-first century, Sr. Suzanne feels anyone planning a liturgy doesn't need to compete with television. We are after something else entirely.

"Entertainment or liturgy as theater has no depth to it. It contains flashy, catchy things, like those needed for television," said Sr. Suzanne with a visible shudder. Gimmicks bring liturgy or prayer services down to the level of entertainment.

What Sr. Suzanne calls gimmicks can be actions as well as objects. They may be flawed attempts to get the people's attention. At one parish, the priest rode through the parking lot precariously perched on a donkey on Palm Sunday with families waving palm branches on either side. Although it was innovative, people enjoyed a bit of Palm Sunday comic relief — Would he slip? Would the donkey jerk to a stop? Were they going inside? — rather than preparation for liturgy.

Even though she has a great sense of humor, Sr. Suzanne's style is, of course, much less boisterous, as fits a retreat center and Motherhouse chapel. She serves as a combination sacristan, liturgist, musician, and administrator of the chapel. She arranges the environment and plans the liturgies. Most of what happens there expresses her style and her intuition about what touches the human spirit. She acts as a kind of divining rod for the holy.

People who come to participate rely on the quality of the Mercy liturgy. The space has the luxury of monastic quiet. "There is a purity, simplicity, and authenticity to the liturgy here," says Fr. Tom Moran, who has celebrated Mass regularly there since 1996. "Sr. Suzanne has a great sense of that. She sees that less is better than more. Suzanne is a breathing reflection of the spirit of Mercy Center. She is an icon of what people experience when they walk in the door. Great simplicity is critical for good liturgy. Suzanne understands that liturgy brings us into mystery."

The environment in the chapel these days is spare. The flowers could be birds of paradise in a vase on the floor by the altar or a cactus during Lent. At Christmas, several simply lit trees sans ornaments are enough. There is never clutter. Sr. Suzanne claims that the simplicity comes from her lack of skill at arranging flowers. There are of course deeper reasons that are part of her own journey.

For the first thirty-five years of Suzanne's life in Burlingame, the chapel had an elaborate plaster baldachino canopying the altar at the far wall of the sanctuary. The ornate structure dominates photographs of all the Sisters' professions since the Motherhouse was built — perhaps a theological statement about religious life and the inaccessible mystery of the Church. In 1986, a committee including Sr. Suzanne and three other sisters — Sisters Diane Grassilli, Judy Carle, and Celeste Marie Nuttman — decided on radical remodeling in the direction of simplicity.

The baldachino had to come down in the name of earthquake safety, they declared. In fact, the cement structure was so solid it took a week of ear-shattering drilling to remove it. Now a spare wooden Word tower and matching tabernacle soar against the wall, leaving much open space in the center. The movable altar sits between the choir stalls used by the Sisters and the wider community. The high stained-glass windows and the dark wood stalls and pews remain, but the plastic figures at the Stations of the Cross are gone, replaced by wooden crosses.

Sr. Suzanne delighted in the new space. The openness matched her sense of spiritual freedom and gave her room to create an authentic environment for prayer. It was a liturgical "home." But there were political difficulties. "A conservative paper published an article about us that said, 'these people have destroyed our Church and older Sisters are crying.' In fact several members of the congregation were upset," she admitted. "One insisted that we keep sections of the pillars. We kept them in the basement for a year and then threw them out."

Firm about her own principles, she has kept the space spare. She changes what hangs on the wall where the altar used to be. During Advent, a simple woven hanging proclaims the season with an Advent symbol; during Lent a large Taizé cross is the sole symbol; during Easter, a large icon of Mary Magdalen in the Easter garden hangs on the wall, and in Ordinary Time, a large icon of the Trinity by Rublev. A wood carving titled "Compassion" by Sr. Carmen Sugiyama stands at the side — a beautifully abstract piece with flowing lines. There are no banners; the flowers are few. At Taizé prayer, the cross with candles against the dark are enough. Everything there is carefully chosen to give emphasis to the season but not to distract.

Sr. Suzanne felt that the props we saw in the vestry were gimmicks because "the objects should be symbols strong enough to hold the mystery. You need basically just the cup and the bread for Eucharist."

"Bad art cheapens the mystery," she said firmly. The theme is dear to her. "Avoid the sentimental. There is a difference between good, true sentiment and the sentimental. The sentimental creates a false emotional state. Mary 'on the half shell' in people's front yards is not good art and is inappropriate even though the owner may be devout."

There's an artistic severity to her guidelines. She confesses the early influence of a class she attended at the University of Notre Dame.

"This old professor was an art teacher, and it was the best art class I ever had. He would say with quick disgust — that's gimmicky! Or that's good! He divided all art into romantic and classical. The romantic was loose form, free flowing. Classic would be done with a consciousness of style and form. I'm a classisist," she confessed. "I like plain and graceful."

"When liturgist Alexander Shaia did the Triduum at Mercy Center, he put a simple bouquet of tulips by the font at the Easter Vigil," said Sr. Suzanne. There are no arrangements bursting with color on the altar or purple banners in the sanctuary and certainly no life-sized plaster statue of Christ. For Sr. Suzanne, those tulips created the kind of enchantment Senn was discussing.

Shaia, an author and spiritual director who worked with Suzanne at Mercy Center for several years in the late 1980s creating Triduum retreats, expressed a philosophy Sr. Suzanne shares.

"When the liturgical environment is beautifully simple," he said, "everything there has a craft and aesthetic sense to it. [On Easter morning] one dozen long-stemmed French tulips next to the Paschal candle, the oil of chrism, and the baptistery say it all.

"We go to worship expecting to be told what it is supposed to be about. It depends on Suzanne and Mercy Center, which is dedicated to a contemplative practice, to reverse that. It is about finding the holy in you, not in the externals.

"Worship opens us up to whatever our experience is. A vase of white tulips does not tell us what this moment is about. It brings our attention to what we need to ponder on the way to the holy," said Alexander.

The tulips are a long way from gauzy gold cloth and granite angels for two reasons. They are naturally exquisite, as eloquent as a Russian icon or a beautifully carved Madonna. They are also symbols of the sacred, not distracting decorations. They point beyond the moment and beyond themselves.

Sr. Suzanne's message is basically to get out of the way. Offer a few focal points to the congregation and make them as beautiful as you can manage. They will be a doorway to the holy. Not every liturgical space can have this contemplative eloquence. The issue isn't money, although money for fine art is welcome, but choice. Less is more. We can clear away clutter in the sanctuary or in a hotel conference room.

Sr. Suzanne praised the recent work of the Mercy High School campus ministers. "Both Rita Cutarelli at Mercy San Francisco and Sandy Flaherty at Mercy High School in Burlingame have a wonderful sense of liturgy. Both create beautiful, energetic liturgies that are at the same time experiences of the holy."

She was fascinated by the authenticity of a recent Mass at the San Francisco high school created by Rita and her students: "A student dance group in long white dresses did the setting of the Mass table. It was so prayerful that you absorbed the beauty of it. The student community understood that 'they are preparing the table' without being told to be quiet. Their attention was riveted there, concentrated on their preparation, not on the fact that the girls were dancing. Art doesn't call attention to itself. It is itself artless."

The key? She paused, and then said, "Something that simple only comes with a lot of preparation. You need to allow the symbols to speak: the altar, the tower of the Word, the tower of the Eucharist, the vessels and the vestments, the cup and the bread."

Through the enchantment of liturgy the story of faith is focused, etched again in memory, and brought to life.

Taizé West Begins

Taizé music is neither silence nor talking. It speaks to me. I had been yearning for a place where music would be a means for delineating sacred space.

—Travis Culwell, attendee of Taizé at Mercy Center

In the 1970s, Sisters no longer had to leave the grounds in twos and could venture out to evening meetings. Sr. Mary Celeste Rouleau went further. In 1977, she traveled to Taizé, France, where an ecumenical community founded in the late 1940s was drawing youthful crowds. The Taizé Brothers created liturgies of simple chants and silence. They wanted worshipers to directly experience God, not just hear others talk about God. Sr. Mary Celeste brought a phonograph record of the songs home to Sr. Suzanne.

Listening to the record in the Motherhouse was a revelation which was to affect Sr. Suzanne's music and her spirituality for the rest of her life. On the record were what she calls "the old chestnuts" of Taizé in Latin: "Laudate Dominum" and "Veni, Sancte Spiritus." She didn't do anything immediately.

"I listened to it and felt, 'That's my music,'" said Sr. Suzanne. "It really touched me. It was so prayerful, so gentle. We had shown a documentary about Taizé to the high school students. I remembered the beauty and transparency of a Brother who spoke about their life together. It was really lovely."

The composer was as usual more than fully occupied. Her *Living Spirit* album had been published by GIA in 1970 with seventeen hymns and psalms. In 1981 Resource Publications published *Keeping Festival*, a record, cassette tape, and music book.

Through the 1970s, she had continued composing, at least a song for each senior class sung at graduation. She collaborated with her biological sister Sr. Patricia in writing *An American Time Capsule*, which included stirring quotes from American history set to music by Suzanne. It ended with Martin Luther King Jr.'s "I Have a Dream" speech. She set Charles Péguy's poem "Hope" to music and at Mission Santa Clara produced a multimedia production of the poem, which included dance and colorful slides.

She composed easily but not confidently. She was directing a choir of students at St. Patrick's Seminary in Menlo Park and learning to write for male voices. Sometimes she used a concordance to string together Scripture verses on a theme. She was never sure if students would like a piece until they tried it out, but having groups to compose for was a great stimulus. As she composed, she continued her other work as well.

From 1981 to 1983 she balanced teaching chorale at the high school with overseeing the growing pains of Mercy Center as the Mercy community sought to figure out which people they could best serve. Sisters Judy Carle and Jean Evans traveled separately to the Taizé community in 1981, joining hundreds of other young people who flocked to the Brothers in southeastern France. They were so enthralled by the simplicity and integrity of the Brothers' lives that the two asked them if the Brothers would come to Burlingame.

"The Brothers came to visit us in 1983 and held several Taizé prayer services around the Bay Area as part of the Taizé 'Pilgrimage of Trust,'" said Sr. Suzanne. "There wasn't a big attendance, but it was a beginning."

Sr. Jean Evans conducted the first Taizé prayer service in the chapel. Sr. Jean has a powerful, resonating soprano that filled the chapel for the chants. Fifteen people came to the first service.

Over the next months. Sr. Suzanne collected musicians—including Sr. Marguerite on the violin—and began to hold regular Taizé prayer services at the Motherhouse chapel on the first Friday of the month. The musicians clustered around her piano in a corner of the chapel.

She was the cantor in the candlelit dark, her high, precise voice beginning "Come and Fill Our Heart With Your Peace," chanting the words to the simple melody. Her singing rose in descant above the phrases as they were repeated, adding a layer of pulse and melody. After several songs to center the assembly, there was a Scripture reading, then silence, the center of the prayer. Sr. Suzanne timed the movements by her finely tuned instinct and her observation of the people. Fidgets and coughs were a clear sign to move on.

Much of the Taizé music is by Jacques Berthier, organist and choir director of St. Ignatius Church in Paris. He and Brother Robert collaborated on writing ostinato responses and chorales, litanies, acclamations, and canons. At first the music was all in Latin, which Sr. Suzanne has said "is a language in which everyone is equally uncomfortable." Now the words are in many languages, which helps explain their international appeal.

Suzanne began to compose in Taizé style. Some of her pieces are usually included in the Mercy chapel service: "Jesus Christ, Yesterday, Today and Forever," "The Will of Your Love," and "Jesus Christ, Inner Light."

"When I first introduced this prayer to groups in the Bay Area and in other places, I sometimes cut the silence a bit short because people are so uneasy with it," wrote Sr. Suzanne in a 2002 article in *The Journal of the Mercy Association in Scripture and Theology* (published by the Sisters of Mercy of the Americas). "But silence, as a resting place with God, is something that grows on us. We find a home for our restless hearts, minds, and bodies."

In 1984, 150 people filled Mercy Center for Taizé prayer with Brothers Leonard, David, and John who came every other year.

Sisters Marguerite Buchanan, Judy Carle, Jean Evans, and Suzanne went with the Brothers to Dominican College in San Rafael and then to Oakland's Holy Names College and a Lutheran church in the East San Francisco Bay area.

"We have wonderful memories of those visits," wrote Brother John, "crowding into Suzanne's car and sometimes driving for fifty miles to lead a prayer service and never knowing exactly what we would find. We also remember with joy the debriefings we had late at night after the days of retreat, or stopping at Fenton's in Oakland to get an ice cream on the way back from a evening of prayer. She did everything she could to make Mercy Center a home away from home for us." In fact, the Brothers began to call Mercy Center "Taizé West."

Brother John didn't explain the debriefings. "At the end of one long day I asked the Brothers to gather with us in the community room for a debriefing," Sr. Suzanne remembered with a smile. "They nodded solemnly. When they arrived, they were delighted to find that it meant chatting over wine and cheese."

Numbers grew as Sr. Suzanne, with the help of Sr. Marguerite, held the Taizé service faithfully every first Friday. Soon over three hundred people were settling into the silence and the dark, coming up for prayer around the cross that lay on the sanctuary floor. Each placed her forehead on the cross in prayer, unburdening herself in silence, a gesture of relief and communion. As the long line of people wound slowly up to the cross, the music extended and repeated for as long as it took for all to come to the front.

"The music itself is enough," observed composer Barbara Bridge who has worked with Sr. Suzanne. "As a phrase is repeated, it goes in deeper. Suzanne embodies that. At Mercy Center, I did a Taizé service with her. She sits at the piano and just goes. She doesn't worry about how it goes. The freedom is very nourishing."

The prayer is an intimate, contemplative experience. For some, it can be so emotionally powerful that it is frightening. What is this experience of the heart and God? Some are simply uncomfortable with the length of the service, which goes on until everyone has had a chance to go up around the cross.

With a smile, Sr. Suzanne acknowledged that the Taizé style doesn't suit everyone. "Sr. Sophia [Newcomb], one of our more practical Sisters, said to me, 'You sing it once, why sing it over and over again?' Then Sr. Amadeus, ever the organizer, advised us to provide several crosses and then just stop if it gets too long!"

But for hundreds of Taizé faithful, the prayer, in spite of or because of its length, is deeply restorative. Travis Culwell, who lives nearby and regularly attends the prayer service, found it compelling. "[The Taizé experience] is what I was hungry for: to be in a place where I am invited to enter the sacred and just be there. Then I can quiet myself and listen to the voice of God. "

The Mercy Center service regularly ends with the stirring "Jesus Christ, Yesterday, Today and Forever" followed by a quieting "Now in Peace, O Lord, Let Your Servant Go" before the people flood the lobby, greeting Sisters Suzanne and Marguerite and each other.

That lobby greeting has given people a chance to meet Sr. Suzanne. Often they are unaware that she is the composer of the famous "I Am the Bread of Life." Vaughn Wolff remembered when he approached her after having attended several prayer services, reluctantly at first.

"After the service I had the urge to seek out the person who was playing the piano," said Vaughn. "I introduced myself. It was Suzanne Toolan! 'Excuse me,' I said, 'are you the one who wrote "I Am the Bread of Life"? She turned red. I was stunned. I was on cloud nine."

Vaughn found his spiritual home in Taizé prayer. He has been a violinist for the prayer since 1990, amazed at himself, a Protestant, for finding this simple, deep ritual so compelling. He had thought of this reverence for silence as being "Catholic," although Taizé prayer is not a Catholic ritual, but an ecumenical one.

"I don't idolize Sr. Suzanne," said Vaughn, despite being overwhelmed when he first met her. "One of the funny things I remember early on was that when she got a drink of water, she said, 'This is pure gin,' and she set it on the piano. What comes through is her humanity. She doesn't allow that 'religious' stuff to get in the way.

"She also doesn't try to orchestrate the musicians. We come together with our different abilities, and we all participate in coaching each other. Before the service she asks us to take different parts. At one time, when I was unfamiliar with a piece, she shrugged her shoulders and said, 'Do what you can.' She is not a perfectionist, but she relies on the spirit and the ability of the person."

Her skill as a composer and her prayerfulness fitted her perfectly for the role she assumed with Taizé. "It was Suzanne Toolan who first understood the power and the beauty of the Taizé experience," said Frank Brownstead, director of music for the Los Angeles Cathedral of Our Lady of the Angels. "A lot of people dabble in Taizé. They have it once in a while. She was able to nourish and foster an ongoing Taizé that people came to count on. She mirrors the French experience, its ecumenical, nonjudgmental aspect. And she is so darn creative she can't help herself."

Sr. Suzanne was in demand to give workshops on Taizé. "When we first started I went out five nights a week during Lent doing Taizé, often in the East San Francisco Bay area," said Sr. Suzanne. "These places weren't necessarily Catholic." Being "geographically dyslexic," as she put it, each such experience was a new opportunity to get lost. She was famous for trying to figure out a map with a flashlight in the car. Grace seemed to protect her.

Once at an East Bay parish over the Bay Bridge and miles from Burlingame, a man lurked up front, drawing close to her at the piano. As ushers tried to shoo him away, he hissed, "Let me be. She's left her wallet. I need to give her money to get back over the bridge." Sr. Sophia had found her wallet in the Motherhouse parking lot and had called the parish. The lurking figure was a parishioner deputized to help an oblivious Sr. Suzanne.

As a reflection of Sr. Suzanne's own constancy, the Taizé prayer service at the Motherhouse chapel has taken place every first Friday of the month without fail since it began in 1983, even if the date were the Fourth of July or a World Series game. Probably no other place in the United States, at least on the West Coast, has continued Taizé prayer with such regularity.

Taizé has given Sr. Suzanne many gifts. "I think that my experience with the music and prayer of Taizé has begun to help me to pray in simplicity. And my experience of the community of Taizé has helped me go beyond myself to embrace the world in all its complexity, in all its needs. In the end, I think my Taizé experience is helping me become a better Sister of Mercy."

She also needed a key to unlock the beauty of congregational singing when she no longer had trained choruses to write for. Taizé provided that key.

SEVEN

Prayer Embodied in Sound

*I wept at the beauty of your hymns and canticles and was
powerfully moved at the sweet sound of your church singing;
the sounds flowed into my ears, and the truth streamed into
my heart.* — St. Augustine of Hippo, *The Confessions,* IX, 6

♫ Sr. Suzanne struck the singing bowl, and the pulses reverberated through the chapel. It was 6:30 a.m., still
winter-dark, and a few figures rustled into the pews and
folded themselves down onto meditation benches. Wood
creaked. She sounded the bowl again and again, waiting each
time for the sound to be absorbed in the dark space and into
our bodies. There was no rush. Her pauses invited the listen-
ers to relish the deep reverberations until they disappeared.
She began a simple chant before the silence of morning
meditation.

In its most basic, music is just this — an arrangement of
sounds and silences. Sr. Suzanne was "playing with" the tools
she's used all her life. These elements tie her to Stravinsky
and to Crosby, Stills, and Nash. These reverberations relate
her work to African drumbeats.

As a composer, she is alert to pure sound as an element
of the holy. In the 1980s, Fr. Tom Hand, SJ, who brought
Christian Zen meditation to Mercy Center, also introduced
her to the chakras, the ancient Hindu system of energy centers in the body. He sounded the centers in preparing people

for meditation, naming each one of the seven with its sound, activating these energy centers from the base of the spine up the body. She was intrigued.

As a good Catholic girl already in the convent in the 1960s, she hadn't experimented with tie dye or any of the Eastern religions, but Fr. Hand's openness to Eastern practices as a way to a more profound Christianity attracted her. She began experimenting with the sounds.

She led interns in Mercy Center's program on spiritual direction through the chakras in a meditation and noticed that concentrating on energy centers in the body was deeply quieting. Her next step led to mixed results.

In giving workshops for pastoral musicians, she often warmed up the audience by leading them through a hymn or vocalizations. At one workshop she decided to present the chakras, as a way of honoring "our human bodies, those great resonating chambers of sound," she said in her opening remarks.

She took the group through the seven chakras from the base of the spine to the forehead, noting the qualities of each and making the sound for each center. Even post-Vatican II, the musicians probably felt this exercise to be wildly experimental. It might have reminded them of an ashram in Berkeley, but most went along.

She noticed that several people in the audience looked tense. A small group sat holding hands tightly, their faces grimacing. Afterward, one of them came up to her and hissed, "You let the evil one in through your talk." Sr. Suzanne nodded and said softly, "Oh, is that so?"

Over twenty years later, she chuckled about it. Actually her theological base was quite firm. The body is a "great resonating chamber of sound." It's one of the basic materials for prayer.

As any singer knows, music glorifies the senses; it is embodied prayer. "Music is made of human stuff," she said at Mt. Angel. "It is created from human breath — it's pulsed and rhythmic like our heartbeat. Song especially is carried by breath. Breath is our connection to God." The chakras are breath and body sounding together.

Most church music may be more dignified than heavy metal bands, but it is still a sensual medium. It is an expression of incarnation. We need bodies to enjoy music. Music invites our hearts to beat more quickly, our feet to tap. "Then sings my soul, my Savior God to thee" stirs us up with exuberant spirit.

One of Sr. Suzanne's themes is that to become more holy we need to become more human, not more abstracted from life. At a Lenten day of Prayer, she quoted Thomas Merton's idea that holiness is not a matter of becoming less human, but more human, more compassionate, more loving, more sensitive to beauty around us. Her theme that day was this: "Lent is a time to become more like Christ, the most human of all beings. He was loving, full of integrity and justice, a man of peace."

In her recent recording *Meditations on the Life of Christ*, Sr. Suzanne improvised evocative pieces that depict Christ skipping through town as a child, later carrying the cross and being mourned by his mother. Charming and sensitive, the pieces skillfully combine her improvisational ability and her sense that Christ had a body with all its freedoms and pains.

Sr. Suzanne invites us to be aware of our bodies, of what makes us happy, or what distracts and distresses us. She speaks about a variety of "prayways." "Sit in a way that is comfortable for you. Let your body relax," she instructed on a retreat day. The body is part of the experience, not something to be fought.

In the same way, she has a sense of the body's involvement in liturgical music. As the psalmist invites us to "Taste and See! How Good the Lord is!" Suzanne has invited liturgical dancers, an Irish harpist, mandolin players, guitarists, and singers of all sorts to be expressive parts of the Mass.

The Church is good at inviting the senses; it is sensual in the truest sense. "Smells and bells" at least on special occasions are a glorious part of liturgy as an art form. What is more softly sensual than candlelight? Or more enlivening than a rousing hymn with the bass line thundering away and the sopranos arching the melody? Music awakens the senses, opening the emotional and spiritual heart to God.

MUSIC FROM ENERGY

Sr. Suzanne found that using the sounds connected with the chakras, or energy centers in the body, was invigorating for musicians. She gave this talk at Mt. Angel Seminary in Oregon in the early 1980s.

A very basic and ancient form of "sound prayer" comes to us from India. To prepare us to sing holy music, we can start, as any good instrumentalist does, by tuning up our instrument — our human bodies, those great resonating chambers of sound. This prayer will take a little time, but I present it as one way that in the busy lives we lead, we can come to stillness and know God.

According to Indian teaching, there are seven major energy centers in the human body. These centers are situated in parts of the body from which activity originate. Energy radiates out of these centers as from the spokes of a wheel. Since "wheel" in Sanskrit is chakra, the energy centers are called chakras. Attention to the seven energy centers can transform a person's life of prayer because it provides a way of "re-collecting" all of one's dissipated and obstructed powers, and submitting them to the integrating power of the Holy Spirit.

Sound is very important in Hindu thought; it is said to be the first vibration of Divine Consciousness. Sound is formed by the vibration of energy, and the basic sound connected with each energy center is called a seed mantra. By uniting the seed mantra sound with the respective chakras, we restore the center to its natural order. Thus, one's whole being is tuned and readied for the player.

If we are to bring these seven energy centers into prayer, it is necessary to know the general area of the center in the body, the types of activity connected with each center, and the seed mantra that corresponds to them.

1. The first chakra is situated in the base of the spine. From it emanates materializing power (imagery), reproduction, and memory. Its negative activities are lust, laziness, and living in the past. Its mantra is *Lam*.

2. The second chakra is centered in the abdomen. From it comes the creative use of the imagination, moderation, and transformation of sexual forces. Negative activities associated with this chakra are uncontrolled imagination, temptation, and untamed sexual yearning. Its mantra is *Vam*.

3. The third chakra is entered in the solar plexus. It too is an emotional center, but a "hot" emotion. From it arises useful anger, persistence, courage, and the ability to laugh. On the negative side are destructive anger, resentment, bitterness, and hostility. Its sound is *Ram*.

4. The fourth chakra is the heart center. We associate this with "warm" emotions, devotion, and compassion. On the negative side are attached love and anxiety. Its sound is *Yam*.

5. The fifth chakra is located in the throat. It is the will chakra. Its positive activities are surrender of the will and constructive use of speech faculties. On the negative side are willfulness, and destructive use of the power of speech. Its seed mantra used for tuning is *Ham*.

6. The sixth chakra is situated in the brain. From it emanates mental activity, intelligence, constructive concepts and discernment — the mind as a tool of the Spirit. On the negative side are pride of intellect, false self-consciousness, and deceitful concepts. Its sound is *Om*.

7. The seventh is the forehead center. This is the spiritual center — the center of faith. Activities that come from this center are silent prayer and infinitely open attention. Negative activities associated with it can be deep self-centeredness, lack of contact with reality and apathy. The seed mantra used to tune this center is *Aum*.

As you go through the tuning of your body, it is important to keep the spinal column in a restful, straight, natural position to bring your whole self to order and open yourself out to God. You may wish to close your eyes or neutralize them by fixing them on an object. First, become aware of any part of the body that is tense, gently relax that part, especially your shoulders. Concentrate on each area of the chakras as you sound them. Begin by doing each one three times.

Base of Spine	Lam
Abdomen	Vam
Solar Plexus	Ram
Heart	Yam
Throat	Ham
Brain	Om
Forehead	Aum

EIGHT

Expressing the Thirst for God

What an experience of God it has been to facilitate the coming together of mind and heart and voice in some precious moments of making music, of singing texts that express the multiplicity of human emotions: joy, sorrow, sadness, playfulness, exultation. — Sr. Suzanne Toolan*

♫ Suddenly one July, Sr. Suzanne rearranged her office. Now a clean and almost empty desk faced the door; the window onto a green courtyard backlit her work. The file cabinet still stood next to the desk with its photo of herself and her sisters as children on top. The brocade love seat from an old convent parlor was along one wall. There was nothing new in the room, but everything was recycled into a fresh place.

This burst of Sr. Suzanne's energy for office renewal might signal a good time to take a fresh look at an old subject: the vitality of church music.

As we settled into the new arrangement, I told her I had been surprised on a recent visit to a California mission. From the lush courtyard garden, I had glimpsed a nun in a full black habit, making her way in the side door with an odd musical instrument. It wasn't a guitar. She was taking a set of synthesizer drums into the noon Mass. I didn't stay to

---

*Sr. Suzanne Toolan, in *Sacred Journey* (The Journal of Fellowship in Prayer), June 2003.

find out if she was actually playing them herself, filling that ornate old space with a heavy beat.

Horrifying? Or cool and relevant?

Sr. Suzanne chuckled, as if to say, this is how we are in the Church, surprisingly human and unpredictable. She was tactfully silent for a moment. I knew she couldn't directly criticize her fellow woman religious who was probably a musician.

As she considered her response, I thought about how quickly others have pounced on the opportunity to give opinions.

What's the point of having any music in the liturgy? Does everyone really have to sing?

Almost everyone who has attended the Catholic Church in the last forty years has an opinion about church music. Some of us yearn for organ music and choirs singing in Latin. Others are sure the St. Louis Jesuits and their successors are geniuses. Some of us would like never to hear another guitar again. Anywhere.

Sr. Suzanne has coached her choirs through difficult anthems and encouraged sleepy Sunday congregations through "Holy, Holy, Holy." In her hundreds of workshops on church music, she makes sure people sing. She draws them in, her right arm stretching high, gracefully gathering the sounds out of the crowd. She wants everyone, even those who were discouraged in the third grade from singing with the group, to experience the magnetic power of music.

She has heard the criticisms. With a slight nod, she acknowledged that she knows Thomas Day in *Why Catholics Can't Sing* * expresses indignation at terrible church music since Vatican II's reforms. He blames a lack of understanding of the role of music and a tolerance of a variety of

---

*Thomas Day, *Why Catholics Can't Sing* (New York: Crossroad, 1992).

aesthetic (and spiritual) sins — egotism, sentimentality, and a repressive attitude about the power of art. He takes aim at contemporary songs, informal priests, and casual choir singing.

No one auditions to be a part of the Body of Christ. We come as we are, tone-deaf or musical. But trained musicians like Day often suffer acutely from the distance between the ideal and limp parish singing.

Sr. Suzanne could join Day's acid perspective on the usual Sunday in what one might call *very* Ordinary Time.

But she's been a relatively unknown pioneer in reaching out to include the people in song. She was one of the first in the American Church to respond to the change of the liturgy to the vernacular mandated by the Second Vatican Council. Her "I Am the Bread of Life" was revolutionary in 1966. Sr. Suzanne used Scripture in English to create a memorable hymn when people were struggling to find something to sing together.

The day we talked she sat back in her desk chair to consider why liturgical music is still a difficult subject, jumping right over the nun and the synthesizer problem.

"I don't think we have a tradition of participation," she said mildly, giving a capsule twentieth-century history of music in the Catholic Church. "For so many years, we were spectators reading the missals, while the priest said something in another language. We read the translation in English on the other side of the page. We were not participating."

In the early 1950s, even vowed women were supposed to just listen respectfully during Mass. Sr. Suzanne began finding ways for the women in the Mercy community to participate. The dialogue Mass, in which the congregation said or sang the responses with the servers, was a start, and the Sisters in Burlingame began to use sung responses in the late 1950s.

As a young nun, Sr. Suzanne became passionate about what the Second Vatican Council later expressed: if the Church is the Body of Christ, congregational music should help knit the members together into a praying community.

She always seemed to have in mind the scriptural basis for the joy of a singing assembly.

> *Praise the Lord.*
> *I will give thanks to the Lord with my whole heart*
> *In the company of the upright, in the congregation!*

> (Psalm 111)

Some of the psalms reverberate with music and invitation to all. The music is spontaneous and effortless, inclusive and exuberant. No choir director stands in the background criticizing the off-key sopranos.

In the twenty-first century, Sr. Suzanne still prepares her Mercy Motherhouse congregation for participating in the Mass. She walks up to the microphone at the lectern, her lanky figure moving carefully now after a second knee replacement. On a recent Sunday, she sang out "Surrexit Christus, Alleluia!" her hands drawing out sound from the assembly. Although this song was familiar to them, she warmed up the congregation of neighbors, Sisters, and retreatants, allowing them to hear their own morning voices.

She demonstrated by even this brief practice that music is not icing on an otherwise drab liturgy. Music is part of the cake, exalting the prayer of the liturgy, bringing it into our senses. Music for her is truly a ministry, as it reflects her own prayer, encouraging others to respond and even guiding their theology.

As we talked that day in her office, Sr. Suzanne paused, fingering a program on her desk from a painful prayer service. A great grief for the community had come with the death that month of Sr. Diane Grassilli, a brilliant leader of the Sisters in Burlingame; she was only 56. The heaviness people felt at her death was almost unbearable. Sr. Suzanne had helped arrange the prayer service for this vital woman, reaching out to people who were feeling bewildered and stunned.

"At the packed prayer service last week for our dear Sr. Diane who was dying," she said, "we sang 'How Can I Keep from Singing?' at the end. There were people there from all threads of her life, all deeply sad. In spite of tears, we sang the words that reminded us of faith:

> *My life flows on in endless song*
> *Above earth's lamentation*
> *No storm can shake my inmost calm*
> *While to that rock I'm clinging.**

"I heard from so many people after the service that the song touched a chord of healing for them. A good hymn is almost instructional. I chose it because its inspiration can lead us out of darkness into light especially in a time like that."

"I have something here," she continued. She opened the file cabinet near the desk and brought out a file from the front. She opened it to show me typed originals of talks she had given over the last fifty years, some on yellowed paper, often with inked-in notes and crossed-out words. These were typed

---

*"How Can I Keep from Singing" copyright © Robert Lowry, GIA, 1992.

before computers. She was casual, as if they were incidental, but they had been carefully kept.

As we quickly checked them over, we saw they contained her thoughts from "Liturgical Music in the Secondary Schools 1958" to "Spirituality and Prayer of the Minister 1995." It was a great collection of resources.

In a 1991 talk to the School of Pastoral Leadership in San Francisco, she said, "There is in every human person a remembrance somehow of who we really are, what we are about. There is in each one of us a deep longing for a relationship with our God. Our lives are busy trying to appease this longing, sometimes looking in strange places for fulfillment. St. Augustine speaks from the depths of his heart and from his experience — and he speaks for each one of us when he says, "Our hearts are restless until they rest in Thee, my God." We are always trying to recover that original completeness, that original bliss, that deep union for which we are made."

As I read over the notes, I saw more clearly that music is a spiritual practice and theology for Sr. Suzanne. Her talks point us in the direction of the meaning of music and liturgy, but her music expresses what and how she believes more transparently even than fifty years of workshop words she has written. Her music gives voice to a longing for God's presence.

"Let's look at some of the music itself," I said. She went to the long, deep closet alongside the office and found a copy of the sheet music for *Living Spirit,* a 1971 collection of her songs.

We leafed through the songs that are favorites with those who were novices and alumnae of her high school chorale. "Stilled and Quiet Is My Soul" expresses longing and its fulfillment in intimacy with God. "I wrote this for our entrance group of sisters in 1966," she explained. "We had been in more than ten years. We were a motley crowd, most of us nonsingers. The theme of our summer was 'presence,' and the song is expressive of God's intimate presence."

> *Stilled and quiet is my soul;*
> *In his presence I take my rest.*
> *O Lord, you have probed me and you know me;*
> *You know when I sit and when I stand;*
> *You understand my thoughts from afar*
> *With all my ways you are familiar.**

Her best known piece, "I Am the Bread of Life," is based on a spiritual hunger expressed as a physical need:

> *You who come to me shall not hunger*
> *You who believe in me shall not thirst*

"Thirst is a way of expressing longing," she said. "My whole being, the whole of humankind thirsts for the living God. Something real. Opening up all that *is*, to the mystery of God."

Musicians especially know how music can both express and create this longing for God in ways that words alone can not. Music is not embellishment; it's essential. It's a way of remembering who we really are, of tapping "our deepest desires," and expressing our deepest desires is praying.

"Some of my most beautiful experiences of God have been in music. I have had lovely notes from students saying it was through music they came to know God," she said, remembering her years as a high school choral conductor. "I could sense it when conducting some times. There is something so wonderful about voices blending, something more than the

---

*"Still and Quiet Is My Soul," GIA copyright © 1966.

notes. The voice is coming from the depths of your human-ness. All of that is pulled together in 'this moment.' Music is embodiment. It uses what is most human about us, our body as resonating chamber. One's deepest soul is expressed in sound. Out of this apparatus come such beauty from the depth of humanity, mind and heart." She rounded her fingers as if she were gently encircling a ball, or perhaps the world.

"It is lovely to see a painting that captures beauty. You can come back to it, but music is in the moment only. It is in the moment that God is."

In the moment. Music touches the holy. Fleeting, evanescent and occasionally glorious. Holding longing and presence to-gether. The vision makes us look again at what we are trying to achieve in choosing a new "Gloria" or going back to a seasoned gathering hymn. Refreshment of the soul is the art. Music evokes prayer from the most stolid heart.

A word others like to use in describing Sr. Suzanne's own music is "authentic." "I Am the Bread of Life" and "Stilled and Quiet" are direct, simple, and well made, like a Shaker chair. The music goes beyond itself to open us up to the mystery of God.

Her fellow composer and musician Sr. Helen Gilsdorf ob-served that "Authenticity is behind Suzanne's desire to having liturgy that is correct and true. She doesn't want false, surface things. It is the authentic union of spirit and body in prayer that makes the difference."

"How do you plan for what will open us up to the mys-tery of God?" I asked. Sr. Suzanne began, "Providing music that will lead to quality prayer presupposes that we as music ministers have come to know our assembly — our parish-ioners — their ethnic backgrounds, their education, their likes and dislikes, where they are musically and spiritually."

Sr. Suzanne admitted, "We probably have to live with the fact that many communities are going to choose to pray with a level of art that leaves someone else in despair."

As a composer and musician, she feels the weight of responsibility always to give people the best possible musicianship, text, and music as a matter of respect. Her own style has evolved into a quietly contemplative grace. Realistically she recommends a variety of music to keep liturgies alive. "Mix styles. Why does everything from beginning to end have to be folk, Renaissance, or rock — or have to be choir, or have to be baroque?"

The mystery of God reverberates for us in good pieces for synthesizer drums, excellent mariachi singers who perform with heart, or fine Gregorian chant.

In the car on the way home, I put *Living Spirit* in the CD player to hear the voices embrace the text:

> *My whole being thirsts for God,*
> *The living God.*
> *How long till I come*
> *And see the face of God?**

Music is about hunger and satisfaction. One's deepest soul expressed in sound. Evanescent. Unpredictable. In the moment.

---

*"Living Spirit, GIA copyright © 1966.

CHOOSING MUSIC FOR LITURGY

What you are striving for in choosing music for the liturgy is an authenticity that communicates in whatever style you are using. Shabbiness, glitz, or sentimentality gets in the way. That's because sentimentality is often very self-indulgent. It keeps us at the surface of our emotions rather than delving deep.

Delving deep lifts up the experience, shares threads of meaning with an audience. Bad art gets in the way of our experience of the holy; it attracts attention to itself rather than to God.

1. **Choose hymns that people can pray with.** The songs can be vigorous, consoling or challenging but should be of good form and easy to sing. What is well-composed form? For example, Marty Haugen's "Song at the Center":

   From the corners of creation
   To the center where we stand
   Let all things be blessed and holy
   All is fashioned by your hand
   Brother wind and sister water
   Mother earth and father sky
   Sacred plants and sacred creatures
   *Sacred people of the land.**

   The melody is simple and easy to follow because of the amount of repetition. Lines 1, 2, and 4 are the same melody. Line 3 contrasts. The repetition gives the congregation a chance to quickly learn the song, so it's a very good form for Sunday singing.

---

*"Song at the Center," Marty Haugen, GIA copyright © 1993.

2. **Repeat songs until people are comfortable with them.** Do this even though you as a musician may be bored with the pieces. It's hard for the congregation to feel prayerful if they are stumbling over notes and words. Complex works aren't appropriate for the assembly. Remember that their only rehearsals are the Masses themselves.

3. **Choose an example of something that touches the moment.** The more directly the hymn can name what is going on in the parish and the world, the better. The hymns should reflect what people are feeling, whether it is the beauty of a spring day, a crisis of war, or the sadness of loss. For example, Brian Wren's piece "When Grief Is Raw":

> *When grief is raw*
> *And music goes unheard*
> *And thought is numb*
> *We have no polished phrases to recite.*
> *In Christ we come*
> *To hear the old familiar words:*
> *"I am the resurrection. I am the life."**

Wren obviously has a gift for directness. He doesn't gloss over the pain of grief but after acknowledging that reality, reminds us of the message of faith.

4. **Pick music that is appropriate for that moment in the liturgy.** "Come, Ye Thankful People, Come" is fine for gathering but not right for the recessional.

---

*"When Grief Is Raw," GIA copyright © 2003.

The communion song should speak specifically about Eucharist; the gathering song can be much more general. The closing song should be vigorous but not too long. People tend to want to get going.

5. **Different modes of music are appropriate in a service.** A fortunate liturgist or musician can offer a variety of music at a service.

1. People can participate by singing themselves.

2. They can listen to others do more complicated things than they can do. If you can train a choir or hire a soloist for occasions, people can participate by listening to excellent, rehearsed music. Instruments and a choir are sometimes best choices. On the other hand, a service that is sung only by a beautiful choir becomes an invitation to passivity. Most composers these days offer a choir part for a hymn with a part for the assembly as well. Don't let the choir always substitute for the voice of the people.

As music publishers know well, foretelling what pieces will become favorites for people is not a science. Congregations are unpredictable, and successful music is somewhat of a mystery. Alice Parker in the magazine *Today's Liturgy* (Lent/Easter Triduum/Easter 2006) said, "A hymn will not survive unless there is a rightness to the words and tune and to their combination, which is more than the sum of their parts. They linger in our memories and inspire us to new connections in our mind and new apprehensions of the Spirit."

Musicians and liturgists offer, and the people decide.

Bringing Contemplation
to Church Music

*Suzanne Toolan understands that liturgy brings us into mys-
tery. The form, the ritual — its words and action — express the
mystery of God which transcends understanding.*

—Fr. Tom Moran

In 1983, Sr. Suzanne suffered a sharp loss familiar to composers. She had no group of singers to compose for. She
retired from her high school teaching and no longer had trained
young voices ready to blend into four-part harmony. Her singers
were now the varied congregation that began appearing on the
Mercy campus. Groups meeting at Mercy Center attended Sunday
Mass, and neighbors came in search of a quiet service with the
promise of good music. She began to turn her attention away from
harmony to writing simpler melodies for ordinary singers similar
to her breakthrough "I Am the Bread of Life."

In spite of the gap left by her chorale, she was busy. In the 1980s
and 1990s, she became a combination housemother, mother superior, expert, and icon of pastoral musicians. "When she is invited
to speak at an National Association of Pastoral Musicians convention," said the late Nancy Bannister, director of the western office
of NPM, "she knows most of the people are struggling pastoral musicians, not getting paid enough, not appreciated, have to fight for
what they need to buy. She understands what a person working for
the Church is up against."

She had a chance to demonstrate that she doesn't take herself seriously. At the NPM meetings in 1980, an after-hours beer and wine party for the planning committee was held, recalled Nancy. "Each person had a hymn parody to sing. Suzanne sat there with a glass of wine in her hand. To the tune of 'I Am the Bread of Life' we sang, 'I am a pastoral musician / I have worked here for twenty-five years / I get five dollars a Mass / for my wife and seventeen kids / my mother-in-law and her cats / and we will starve to death / for the glory of God.' All joined in at full voice. We looked at Suzanne. She was laughing out loud with her head thrown back with her glass toasting us."

On the local level, Linda Myers at St. Isabella's parish in Marin County north of San Francisco was grateful for Suzanne's help during a workshop for everyone involved in the parish liturgy — ushers, cantors, lectors, and musicians. "She makes people think they can do it and don't have to be professional," said Linda. "She instills confidence in people with a gentle way that is unique to her. The point is to get the lady in the pew to sing out. When Sr. Suzanne sings, everyone is going to sing. She raises those hands and you do!"

For a period, diverted by her Mercy Center role and suffering from a lack of trained singers to write for, she wasn't publishing much music.

She was worried about her friend Sr. Marguerite; her concern drew her into creating opportunities for the two to work together. Sr. Marguerite — an imposing, stately figure with her white hair twisted into a bun, a former biology teacher and later decisive principal at the Mercy High Schools in San Francisco and Burlingame — is a fearless spiritual seeker and in many ways Sr. Suzanne's opposite. Where Sr. Suzanne is reserved, Sr. Marguerite is outspoken. If Sr. Suzanne works alone, intuitively and at the last minute, Sr. Marguerite plans carefully with a team. If Sr. Suzanne's changes are gradual, Sr. Marguerite can swing with breathtaking swiftness to a new idea from Centering Prayer to Bede Griffiths' union of Hinduism and Christianity. Where Sr. Suzanne shies from publicity and confrontation, Sr. Marguerite, unabashedly beaming, buttonholes the world for support of a new project.

In the 1980s, Sr. Marguerite was enrolled in courses in the Institute of Transpersonal Psychology, then in Menlo Park, a few miles south of Burlingame. Sr. Suzanne worried that Sr. Marguerite was falling off the theological edge and maybe out of the Mercy community, but Sr. Marguerite was not to be deterred from her quest.

"At the Institute of Transpersonal Psychology [ITP] a branch of psychology was taught that acknowledges the Divine presence within," said Sr. Marguerite, explaining her studies there. "The deepest layer of consciousness is that of the presence of God, the experience of the meaning of Christ."

"At first, I balked at Marguerite's changes," said Sr. Suzanne, "but I saw that ITP provides a broad base that embraces all spirituality. The full development of the human person is not reached without spiritual development.

But Sr. Suzanne was still concerned about Sr. Marguerite, so she pulled her into giving retreats and workshops throughout the United States. "In these retreats we created a shared experience," said Sr. Marguerite, "giving a psychological framework to the Christian tradition. We did many years of retreats using a transpersonal approach, which is transparent in its understanding of symbols, the unconscious, and access to the Divine. Retreatants were led to deepen their prayer experience through Sr. Suzanne's music, ritual, and silent meditation."

As a result, Suzanne felt her own prayer life move from one focused on the interior to a consciousness of others. "The Church should be a presence that welcomes in the name of Jesus Christ. It is a sign of Christ's presence, reaching out in compassion, especially to the poor," she said, perhaps thinking of songs such as "Weaving Round":

Weave, weave, weave us together
In one great family,
Though many races, cultures, and languages,
We are all one in Jesus Christ.*

She began writing in the Taizé style, with the repeated refrain as the basis for variations sung above it. When the Taizé Brothers were in Burlingame, community founder Brother Roger called from France one afternoon. Sr. Suzanne answered the phone in her office, but, not speaking French, she handed the phone to one of the Brothers. The conversation came around to music. Over the phone, Brother Roger dictated the words to "The Will of Your Love" and "Jesus Christ, Inner Light" for which Suzanne created memorable and haunting settings.

"I like the simplicity, the shortness of line," she said, "but also I love the idea that you can keep adding different textures — the solo descants, the instrumental parts layered over. It doesn't become boring."

When Pope John Paul II came to San Francisco in 1986, she was asked to write for the Mass at Candlestick Park. She composed "Jesus Christ Yesterday, Today and Forever" (published by GIA) in the Taizé style. The rising, triumphant lines are usually part of the ending of Taizé prayer at Mercy Center.

"I've become much more simple," she said in 1998. "Through the Taizé service, I've seen that people can come to a contemplative spirit through repetitive, mantric music. It deepens until it is really lectio divina, which is a reading of the Word and mulling it over. You lose touch with the Word itself as it becomes an undercurrent of prayer in which words are not important. Thoughts are not predominant. What is important is deep connection to the Divine."

The Taizé style has also influenced the way she prepares liturgy. Even Fr. Tom Hand, SJ, was sometimes puzzled by her lack of verbal directions in the Mass. "She doesn't like explanations. She thinks the liturgy should explain itself," said Fr. Tom. "But as a celebrant at a weekday Mass for the community, you sometimes wonder what will happen next. I wonder a lot of times, am I supposed to sing this? Or do that? Am I supposed to handle the Alleluia or is she? I got used to asking because those things could get lost."

Another encouragement for her was that she again attracted the attention of a publisher.

In the early 1990s, composer Bob Hurd attended Eucharist at the Mercy Motherhouse. Then teaching at the Franciscan School in Berkeley and familiar with her music, he was curious about what Sr. Suzanne was writing. He approached her after Mass.

Anyone who has ever met Sr. Suzanne even for an instant senses her shyness, the first tentativeness of her words. But she has an instinct for hospitality as strong as her instinct for good music. Sr. Suzanne's face lit up when she heard who Bob was.

"She knew my work," said Bob. "We started talking about music in general. I became aware that she was writing a lot of music and putting it into a drawer. She played the pieces for me and then would say they were not any good. They were gorgeous."

Bob called his publisher, Oregon Catholic Press, and told Paulette McCoy, then in charge of the music division, of his discovery. He thought Paulette could persuade Suzanne to open that musical drawer.

Delighted with what she found, Paulette knew how to work with a reticent composer who never appreciated her talent enough. As a publisher, she was excited about the flexibility and range of the music Sr. Suzanne was persuaded to show her. "Suzanne has ability to write for quite a wide audience, both sophisticated choral music and beautiful yet simple ostinato refrains," Paulette said.

"The beauty of her music is the marriage of text and music. She is a phenomenal composer and musician."

Sr. Suzanne sometimes belittles her music because it is not "extroverted" like that popular today in many parishes. Mercy Center faithful Travis Culwell disagrees with her. As a musician himself, he finds the quality of her music, written in an ageless style, sustains him. "I feel that her ministry brings me a sense of the completely current and contemporary," said Travis. "The music is real and accessible. I find her music very exuberant."

Her surroundings, in addition to Taizé, shine through her music. At Mercy Center she has been rooted in a place where people come to reflect, pray, and be silent. The Center is a place of listening and quiet; years of prayers are embedded in the chapel's dark pews. Placid labyrinth circles, redwoods filtering light into Center windows, and the brilliance of cherry trees in spring all persuade the senses of peace.

"Few words draw many," said Fr. Thomas Moran, who has celebrated Mass at Mercy Motherhouse chapel over the last ten years. "People are drawn to monasteries without words. Suzanne is a breathing reflection of the contemplative spirit of Mercy Center. She is an icon of what people experience when they walk in the door."

She wrote that Taizé confirms an intuition she had years ago before she entered religious life: "Where words leave off or become inadequate to express the power of the mystery, there music takes over, expressing a thought or feeling or prayer in a manner beyond words. And where music itself is inadequate, there is silence."

Sr. Suzanne continues to focus on the essence of worship, which is to her the core of consciousness: a sense of God's all-pervading love. Her pastoral task is to bring others to this boundless place.

NINE

Symbols as Power
or Symbols as Doorways?

Days pass and the years vanish and we walk sightless among miracles. Lord, fill our eyes with seeing and our minds with knowing. Let there be moments when your Presence, like lightning, illuminates the darkness in which we walk. Help us to see, wherever we gaze, that the bush burns, unconsumed. And we, clay touched by God, will reach out for holiness and exclaim in wonder, "How filled with awe is this place and we did not know it." *

> *For all the history of grief*
> *An empty doorway and a maple leaf.*
> — Archibald MacLeish, *Ars Poetica*

♫ "Liturgy is an art form, like a poem," explained Fr. Tom Moran. "You identify with the experience of the poet. You become one with what is happening in good liturgy. Suzanne creates that oneness through her preparation of liturgies."

Preparing an art form every Sunday sounds like an intimidating task, but of course no one does it alone from scratch. The Christian tradition overflows with riches. The prayers,

---

*Gates of Prayer, The New Union Prayerbook, Weekdays, Sabbaths, and Festivals; Services and Prayers for Synagogue and Home (New York: Central Conference of American Rabbis, 1975), 373.

readings, and gestures are there, ready for the season. "The work of the people" is also a gift, handed down to be opened again and again.

This "work" is embedded with symbols, from candlelight to the gesture of the kiss of peace. "[The historic liturgy of the church] is freighted with archetypal and primordial symbols of light and darkness, inclusion and exclusion, feasting and fasting that serve to open us to a sense of the sacred," observed Lutheran theologian Frank Senn in *Christian Liturgy.**

Thinking about Senn's comments on the richness of liturgical symbols, Sr. Suzanne and I walked around the Motherhouse chapel to look more closely at what has been her home, a place where she has spent thousands of hours, praying, touching the piano keys, and singing the responses. The chapel reflects her spirit as it reflects the lives of the Sisters who have worshiped here for over seventy-five years.

She and the other Sisters have made the Motherhouse chapel a place of visual calm to aid prayer. The centerpiece changes with the season; when I visit, it is the softly lit icon of the Trinity. Comfortable niches for sitting in prayer on either side invite the visitor.

"The square oak altar, where we celebrate our oneness, looks like the table it represents," she said, as she walked around the space. The vines and grapes carved on the altar repeat on the choir stalls, which are now pews for the congregation. The soaring wood frames holding the tabernacle and the Word on the front wall repeat the Gothic arches of the chapel ceiling itself. Even the doors bear the same graceful curving shape.

What do these visual touches do for the liturgy?

---

*Frank Senn, *Christian Liturgy* (Minneapolis: Augsburg Fortress, 1997), 704.

The comparison with poetry can help us here. As MacLeish suggests in his lines, poetic symbols are powerful because they don't spell out meanings; they can't. They echo realities that can't be contained in an explanation. The "empty doorway" and the "maple leaf" refer us to our own experiences of emptiness and loss. We have empathy for the poet's perspective because he invites us to revisit our own. We are there with him in the doorway.

In the same way, a true liturgical symbol reverberates beyond itself in the heart and mind of the observer. "The liturgy is full of symbols: the table facing the people, the cross, candles, bread and wine, the vestments, the Scriptures," said Sr. Suzanne.

Symbols lead us out of our isolated selves, bringing the past present and carrying us into the holy.

"For it is the very nature of symbol that it reveals and communicates the 'other' as precisely the 'other,' the visibility of the invisible as invisible," said Orthodox theologian Fr. Alexander Schmemann in *For the Life of the World*.*

But Sr. Suzanne doesn't rely on theological explanations; she has an instinct for what reveals the sacred reality, the "other" in the chapel environment. Not every statue or ancient cross satisfies her. "The object must be able to hold the meaning, or it is not a symbol,"she said. Stone cherubs and glittery cloth are not adequate.

What "holds the meaning"? Sr. Suzanne and I discussed a carefully chosen carved stone Madonna I saw at a retreat house. Set on a low table, the small curving figure had no detail, only lines which suggested the cupping of a hand or the encircling motion of the heart. It bent over a round object, embracing it.

---

*Fr. Alexander Schmemann, *For the Life of the World* (New York: Athens Printing Company, 1988), 141.

The figure suggested loving protection, vulnerability, connectedness, and motherhood. It drew me, calling on my own feelings and experiences of being both a mother and a child. But it pointed beyond those to the holiness of Mary and her child and the universality of this tenderness. The abstract Madonna was a powerful example of MacLeish's "empty doorway" and "maple leaf."

In that same retreat house chapel beyond the figure was an icon of the Madonna on the altar, echoing the small carving. The placement of the two enlarged their individual intentions. There was prayerful authenticity and artistic craft in both the icon and the sculpture.

Sr. Suzanne agreed that these Madonnas could "hold the meaning." They call the observer back again and again with some new dimension of prayer or intuition, like great paintings that reveal new truths on each viewing or great books whose levels are peeled away with each reading.

The environment of the Motherhouse chapel is disarmingly simple. Sr. Suzanne is allergic to plastic crucifixes or factory-produced Madonnas. The vessels, the cross, and any decorations must be carefully chosen and of good workmanship. Statues and pictures are not just helpful images suggesting beloved figures to our imaginations; they represent the layers of the sacred burning through: "how filled with awe is this place and we did not know it."

In the changing fashions of church decoration, we inherit sanctuaries sprinkled with venerable plaster statues with coy smiles and garish coloring. We don't agree on what good art is, and most of us in a congregation are, at best, amateur art critics.

Sr. Suzanne outlined a few of the principles she uses in choosing symbols:

* Simplify to focus on the symbols that are there. Don't allow the sanctuary to look as if a Hollywood set was raided to furnish it, even for a special celebration. Reduce clutter as you can. Unless a symbol can speak for itself, it is not doing its job. If the liturgist or pastor has to talk about what it means, it isn't effective.

* Use repetition of symbol, shape, and color to create a feeling of unity and calm.

* Pay attention to what makes the parishioners feel at home. The spirit and aliveness of the parish is more important than rigid artistic standards. We need to welcome symbols familiar to other cultures — the Virgin of Guadalupe and her cape, for example.

Like silence and music, visual symbols open us to what is wordless. The symbolic action of gesture expresses our own silent participation in prayer.

Carlo Busby, director of Mercy Center from 1997 to 2000, wrote eloquently about the symbolic gestures Sr. Suzanne fosters in her liturgies and prayer services:

> The power of gesture prompted me to think of the way gesture plays such an important role among us at Mercy Center; each gesture is a different way of expressing a hope, a prayer, a longing that is often beyond our words. Kneeling in prayer, sitting in meditation, silently walking the Labyrinth, bowing before the cross during Taizé prayer, signing with holy water, genuflections, greetings of peace, blessings of oil, and even the silent facial gestures of attentive listening — all gestures of reverence, revealing to us and bringing us into the presence of God's grace.*

*Carlo Busby in *Highlights* newsletter (Burlingame, CA: Mercy Center, Fall 1999).

Mercy Center Opens

It is our hope that Mercy Center will respond effectively to the growing spiritual needs of our time and will provide a means for us to share with God's people the spiritual, personal and material resources with which we have been blessed.

—Sr. Rosemary Sullivan, Superior General,
Sisters of Mercy Burlingame, September 1981

The Motherhouse convent was buzzing. In their living groups, the Sisters were turning an idea over in their minds, and Sr. Suzanne was one of those responsible for this ferment. After their work with refugees or a day discussing a religious education program with a pastor, during dinner and before they graded papers in their narrow bedrooms, the Sisters discussed and debated. It was November 1980, and the clock was ticking on well past Vatican II. Few novices had entered the Mercy community since the mid-1970s, but as usual, the world was raw with spiritual needs.

Sr. Suzanne and several other Sisters had an idea for a bold experiment. The group sent out a questionnaire to the Sisters about how the novitiate space should be used. The ad hoc group presented an idea that to some Sisters sounded scary. The concept was simple and perhaps even obvious: open a retreat center in the mostly empty novice wing.

Thousands of people each year would walk through hallways that had been cloistered convent space. Sisters would move out of their bedrooms. Strangers would freely wander the pathways under the oaks. There would be a financial risk, but as a religious community very much tuned to the world, the Sisters knew the

147

pressing need for a place people could visit for quiet and contemplation. Vatican II had opened the windows of theology and prayer for laypeople. "Vatican II invited everyone to holiness," Sr. Marguerite Buchanan observed. "Parishes don't have the time and space or staff to offer spiritual enrichment. They have to deal with everything from baptisms to problems of the frail elderly."

Sr. Suzanne is also one of the original environmentalists. Brought up in the Depression as well as formed by religious life, she likes to reuse everything. The black candle holders that once stood as sentinels around the casket at a sister's funeral have become plant stands in her office, perfect for holding trailing philodendrons.

She and others were considering "reuse and recycle" on a larger scale. The vow of poverty implies careful use of any gifts you are given, including property. The Coolock Wing of the Motherhouse with its ninety bedrooms built in 1962 was used as a novitiate and juniorate for about ten years. In 1981, only a few Sisters remained in its small rooms. The place needed to have the heat on, the windows opened, and the water run. It needed to be used.

Sr. Helena Sanfilippo surveyed sixteen retreat centers in the Bay Area to evaluate unmet needs. Yes, there were requests that couldn't be met, she found. Mt. Alverno Retreat Center, run by the Franciscan Sisters in Redwood City, especially noted that they had to turn groups away for lack of space.

The Sisters' concern was for ministry needs, first, and utilization of space, second. The General Council, the Sisters' leadership group, made the decision to open a retreat center.

Sr. Suzanne was named director of the new Mercy Center on May 21, 1981. This venture would open doorways that would influence Sr. Suzanne personally in the ways she prayed, in her theology, and in the music she wrote. This change would begin a dynamic new chapter in her life.

Why did she volunteer for this new role? It was an especially daring one for her. If she didn't like to assign her students seats on a bus, how would she assign bedrooms? Would she be able to make difficult decisions about staffing? How would she find it in her heart to charge people for services that she would like to give freely?

What she did have was great empathy for spiritual and emotional needs of people, not just Catholics. She seemed always to be attuned to what a congregation hungered for. Since shortly after Vatican II, when ecumenism had great energy, she had participated in services that offered the promise of Christians coming together. On Good Friday 1967, the Mercy choir sang three of her works at Calvary Presbyterian in San Francisco, "Walk in Light," "Stilled and Quiet Is My Soul," and "Living Waters."

In 1968 she conducted the music for a service at the San Francisco Civic Auditorium planned by the Christian Unity Committee. The music included "I Am the Bread of Life" and her "Hymn of Peace." The Salvation Army Band, Bishop Mark Hurley, and various Protestants joined in the celebration.

She had come a long way from her childhood when she and one of her biological sisters had been terrified at their own boldness in stepping inside a Protestant church in Lansing. "I was trembling afterward," she remembered.

She could sense that the world, or at least the San Francisco Bay Area, needed what the Mercys could offer on their campus. In a letter to parish women in May 1981, she wrote of a complex vision. The Center would be a place for growth activities — retreats, days of recollection, ongoing spiritual direction, workshops in biblical, theological, and psychological areas, as well as for young adult ministry, training for lay leadership. It would be an oasis. It would be a place for experiential activities and for gathering resources, including books, tapes, art, and staff.

The full-time staff was very small at the beginning: in addition to Sr. Suzanne, Sr. Yvonne Folsom served as reservations manager,

Sr. Lourdes Harkness was director of maintenance, and Sr. Marian Curran served as financial director. Other Sisters and laypeople volunteered to help.

Church groups snapped up the offer of space at a reasonable rate. The California Association of Catholic Hospitals inaugurated the Center with their annual meeting in October 1981. Students from Mercy High San Francisco had a silent retreat. Riordan students and faculties of other Catholic schools used the building. An exhibit of serigraphs by Corita Kent lent by graphic artist George Collopy was an artistic highlight.

It was a time for experimenting. Some courses sounded wonderful and then had few participants. The nuns were full of ideas such as "A Day of Jogging and Spirituality," for which only one person signed up. Even an Advent workshop for liturgists and teachers given by the worship committee of the archdiocese with presenters Sisters Jean Evans, Diane Grassilli, and Celeste Marie Nuttman had low attendance.

Not every Sister was happy, and some complained about the constant traffic of newcomers, remembered staff member Sharon Almeida. "Guests would sometimes arrive in the middle of the night without luggage, which had been delayed," said Sharon who began first as a volunteer in 1982. "Sisters would be asked to loan them nightgowns. Suzanne's office was toward the front where the bookstore is now. She had insomnia, so late at night she would be working at her desk and would be up to meet these guests."

Sr. Suzanne had insomnia because she was always worried about the finances. She wrote to the Sisters a month after the Center opened, apologizing for the cost of $22 per day. She expressed surprise that the costs were so high and made a plea for communication with the kitchen about meals.

The source of both the grace and the problems was Sr. Suzanne's deeply felt sense of hospitality. "She really set hospitality as the main characteristic of Mercy Center," said Fr. Tom Hand, SJ, who joined the staff in 1984 to lead the East West meditation program. "It is all connected with Divine Love, Christ. This is her concrete way of manifesting the Mercy charism. I have heard people say that at Mercy Center they feel at home; it is their lighthouse and their life. She set that tone to Mercy Center at the beginning."

Her sense of hospitality was behind her ecumenical welcome. In December 1981, she wrote in the annals, "Not only have its doors been opened wide to all segments of the Catholic society, but ecumenism has also become one of its outstanding marks. Methodists, Episcopalians, Baptists and Presbyterians found their way here during its first year."

She couldn't bear to charge groups that she thought had few resources. In the annals for September 1985, she noted, "In retrospect, the core staff [presumably including Suzanne herself] recognized that Suzanne was too soft on people who canceled reservations, did not come up with minimum numbers, or even *suggested* our prices were too high. The staff found from the first financial statement that they were running in the red. All agreed that Suzanne should have 'Nothing to do with charges.'"

Sr. Mary Waskowiak, who later went on to leadership with the Sisters of Mercy at the Institute of the Sisters of Mercy of the Americas, knew she made Sr. Suzanne very uncomfortable when Mary took over in 1988. "I was too organized," said Sr. Mary. "I would say, here is the price scale. She would say, 'You can't do that. You have to let them have it for free if they can't pay.' A lot of her decisions were made intuitively and from the heart. She had founding charisma."

Her sense of the importance of the Center overrode any doubts she had about how to administer the place. "I wasn't a strong leader, but right away it was a go," said Sr. Suzanne. "We were near the airport and far enough from San Francisco to be a retreat place."

Location was probably the least of the factors. She felt a deep sense of obligation to the nuns to make the Center a success. As always, she worked very hard. She made beds and cleaned the bathrooms when it was her turn to be on duty. She and other sisters set up meeting rooms. "I thought she would die of exhaustion," said Rey Friel, who was Sr. Maria in the convent until 1983. "There was nothing in place."

The foray into administration excited and worried her at the same time. "I was never a real director. My gift was that people came out of the woodwork to help me," she said. Discounting her usual self-doubt, the fact was that many rallied around her. Sr. Mary Eucharia Malone taught her administrative systems. Sharon Almeida, a gifted administrative assistant with great reserves of patience, appeared as volunteer and later staff member. Sr. Marguerite Buchanan signed on in 1983 to do anything needed and became a font of program ideas and her companion in giving retreats.

As a practical director, Sr. Suzanne scavenged for furniture and often "reassigned" it, raiding basement rooms for unused chairs for conference groups and sometimes making do. "We confiscated an oriental rug from the convent front parlor," she deadpanned in the 1986 annals. "It was badly worn, but upside down we find it looks good."

The Center was known in the Motherhouse kitchen as "the Back" and didn't get much priority in services, she felt. They had a janitor twice a week.

She had to learn about the limits of reuse. "We had this lovely handyman who fixed our plumbing with string," said Sr. Suzanne. "Of course, it would break on weekends, so we had floods. Finally it happened at midnight one weekend. I had to call Treasurer General Sr. Lillian [Murphy] who lived here. Lillian, who was like a CFO, gave me her credit card, and said firmly, 'Get service on a monthly basis.'"

She cared deeply about how the environment looked and felt. Her sensitivity made her aware of bad art. When the Center opened in 1981, she removed what she regarded as a "terrible statue of Mary" and took down the plastic crucifixes in the bedrooms for visitors. Another nun discovered Mary in the closet facing the corner "like a bad girl," said Sr. Suzanne with a conspiratorial lilt in her voice. The Sister was outraged, but Sr. Suzanne prevailed as she was, after all, the director. The artistically defective Mary stayed in seclusion. As for the crucifixes, Suzanne said, "We have more reverence for the cross than that to have it in plastic." They were replaced by a print of a sacred masterwork or an icon.

The changes in the chapel reflected the increasing openness and graceful simplicity that she prized. When the carved cement baldachino over the altar came down in 1988, the soaring wood of the ambo and the tabernacle directed hearts heavenward with fewer impediments.

She distributed art throughout the Center from Russell College, the college for the novices and juniors which had closed. The placement of every Madonna, every icon of the Christ Child was important to her. She had always had a sense of discrimination about visual art because the environment made so much difference to her.

In 2006, she and Mercy Center staff member Catherine Wilkinson began to refresh the look of Mercy Center by rearranging furniture and moving around the prints and sculpture. For someone who had taken rugs from the Sisters' parlors to use "upside down" in Mercy Center, the rearrangement was a natural act. Suzanne also had a mental catalogue of every painting, carving, and icon throughout the four floors of the Motherhouse and Center. With great delight, she and Catherine "robbed Peter to decorate Paul," as Catherine said, taking art from bedroom corridors and displaying it to better advantage in more public hallways.

Their goal was first to make the public spaces more welcoming and beautiful without spending money. They rehung icons against a newly painted blue wall in the Maple Dining Room with stunning effect and warmed up the small Willow dining room with Impressionist art hung against a warm gold background.

"Her sense of beauty is austere," said Catherine, "and she has perfect visual pitch." She knows that a Giotto will be complemented by modern art of pastel shapes in the dining room and both will echo the wall of icons. Her sense of placement is unerring.

Outside the artistic field, as director she found that people came to help her with tasks she couldn't do. She invited people to do what they could do well, and she gave them physical and emotional space to do it. If she didn't like to manage, she was skilled at encouragement, and she had the credibility from her musical fame to make it work.

Vatican II had asked that the Sisters reexamine their purpose and rules, which women religious did, many with great energy and thoroughness. As part of the process they began looking inward with contemporary psychological tools; some like the Sisters of the Immaculate Heart in Los Angeles ran at cross-purposes with their archbishop as they became more self-determined, reading contemporary authors, studying theology, and determining what education their Sisters would have.

The Sisters of Mercy in Burlingame were careful not to go too far in the direction of reform. But the renewal not only gave them permission to change but also access to those seeking Christ in a wide variety of ways. Some went to school to get their doctorates in theology. A few studied the Enneagram, a nine-pointed system of understanding one's personality based on an ancient Sufi figure. Others became skilled in energy healing. The fledgling Mercy Housing began finding funding and building affordable housing for the urban poor at this time. Housing became a vibrant ministry which spread from its origins in Omaha to California and other areas nationwide.

As always, Suzanne was willing to try new things. She nurtured programs and practices that became the core of the Center for over twenty years. She worked well with Sr. Mary Eucharia, a dynamite organizer, who had been in community leadership and who had at least one irrepressible new idea every day. Thorough and energetic, Sr. Mary Eucharia researched Scripture programs. Using the model of evangelical Bible study fellowship, she began the Shared Scripture Program that still meets weekly with speakers and discussion groups.

Sr. Mary Eucharia brought the Home Retreat to Mercy Center which still continues today. For one week each summer people still meet daily with a spiritual director and have worship opportunities at the Center while living at home.

"Eucharia is responsible for so much in the Center," wrote Sr. Suzanne in the annals when Sr. Mary Eucharia left the Center in 1986. "Her experience as an administrator, her knowledge and freedom with finance, her great vision and her unbounded energy helped to form this Center and make it the quality place it is."

People wanted to do more than come to programs at the Center. Some wanted to make radical changes. Spiritual direction was slowly growing as a vocation. Helping people listen to the message of God in their lives was a skill laypeople could learn, and many in religious life were attracted to it as well.

Sr. Mary Ann Scofield, who as formation director had helped novices develop their spiritual lives, took on spiritual direction as her ministry. She was trained at the Center for Religious Development in Cambridge, Massachusetts, and with Sr. Janet Ruffing began a program at the Center in 1984. "People seek spiritual directors because they are having experiences of God and don't know where to have them tended," said Sr. Mary Ann, known as one of the founding mothers of the spiritual direction movement on the

West Coast. The internship in spiritual direction developed into a well-regarded program taught with care and skill at the Center.

Sr. Suzanne was uncomfortable doing spiritual direction herself; she admits it is a much-too-intense one-on-one relationship for her. Seeing that many people needed the nurturing that this spiritual "coaching" offers, she encouraged the training program that she counts as one of the most important the Center established.

She became more personally involved in a crucial invitation she made in 1984. She asked a Jesuit who had given a retreat at the Motherhouse in 1977 if he would be interested in joining the staff. Fr. Thomas Hand, SJ, who had studied Zen meditation formally for six years, had just returned from twenty-nine years in Japan and was unsure where his next step would be.

Sr. Suzanne saw the opportunity for hospitality and was drawn to what Fr. Hand had to offer.

"She had a breakthrough in a retreat that I gave six years before I came to Mercy Center, in 1978," said Fr. Tom. "That was one of the reasons she asked me to come. She realized meditation was part of what she wanted."

She had taught novices a class called "Response to the Sacred" that had covered a variety of religions, so Zen meditation was not totally foreign to her. She felt comfortable with this new direction because one of the documents from Vatican II had stated, "Let them reflect attentively on how Christian religious life may assimilate the ascetic and contemplative traditions, whose seeds were sometimes planted by God in ancient cultures already prior to the preaching of the Gospel."*

She understood that meditation brought her great peace and satisfaction. Mercy Center was already known as "solidly based,"

---

*Excerpt from *Ad Gentes,* On the Mission Activity of the Church.

so it could afford a venture into a practice familiar only to a minority of Catholics at that time, although Christian meditation has deep historical roots.

Fr. Tom was more than pleased to accept Sr. Suzanne's invitation to what became a long, final chapter to his life and the opening of a rich and satisfying one for many touched by the Center. He moved into rooms on the basement floor of the Center where he lived until illness forced him to move to the Jesuit Provincial House in Los Gatos, California, in 2004, where he died in 2005.

He brought a combination of a spacious yet disciplined mind and a wonderfully wry sense of humor to the convent. He was an excellent guide and mentor for Sr. Suzanne, but she and other Mercys influenced him as well.

"Tom Hand came and opened us up!" Sr. Suzanne said ebulliently. "I was a narrow Roman Catholic, but he was mind- and heart-expanding. At breakfast, we always had great conversations, settling all political problems.

"We affected him with feminist theology," she said. "All you had to do was to tell him something once and he went much further than one would think. He was very careful about language."

Fr. Tom began to hold retreats at the Center, giving instructions on breathing and concentration as he sat in his black robes on a floor cushion, or "zafu." Many found their way to the sacred through the silences of these retreats.

He began morning sitting in the Motherhouse chapel, which was open to all, in February 1985. People came to sit on the floor on cushions. Some, including Sisters, sat in the pews. To start the forty minutes of silence, he struck a deep gong that reverberated through the dark. After a chant he gave a few words to center the meditators. Sr. Suzanne came faithfully and unobtrusively copied down his words, compiling them into a pamphlet, "Dawn Wisdom," which included these insights:

Meditation is not a retreat from reality but an escape to reality, a return to the Source, a coming home.

When the waters are stilled and quiet, we can see the bottom of the pool. When our minds are stilled, then we can see within where shines the Face of God.

"It was a wonderful emancipation to listen to him morning after morning and break out of a narrow shell," Sr. Suzanne said. "We were rooted in Catholicism, but we expanded our thought to other Christian traditions, then out to Native American, Buddhist, and Hindu spirituality."

Holding the body still and relaxed, focusing the mind on a word or the breath, letting the thoughts go, coming into the holy present, again and again. Silence. Effortless effort.

These were the ways to pray that Sr. Suzanne had been seeking in her early days as a novice when she had sat sleepily in front of a prayer book.

The Center was clearly a success. A composer and musician, with the help of her sisters and volunteers, had successfully created a spiritual oasis on the San Francisco Peninsula. At the same time, they managed the bustle of thousands of people coming through its doors each year. Her own spiritual growth felt the impact.

PRAYER AS RELATIONSHIP

Fr. Thomas Keating likens our relationship to God to human relationship.

1. The first step in any human relationship is acquaintance: It is not a deep sort of thing. I meet someone on the bus corner. I might meet this person every morning, and I exchange greetings. The acquaintance is not deep.

What does this have to do with our relationship with God? Our relationship with God follows the same path. We might regard God just as an acquaintance, one we meet once a week at Mass, but one who does not become a guiding, permeating force in our lives during the week.

2. Drawing on human relationships, we go a step further. From acquaintance, I might become *friendly* with him or her. Now I might be at the stage where I exchange thoughts about the government and how it should be run.

In our relationship with God this might look like this: I begin to listen to that Sunday Gospel a little more closely and remember some of it later. I find myself asking God for things, or thanking God, but the relationship remains rather superficial.

3. With some people a human relationship goes much further. This next step is a big one. I become a *friend* of this person. I have a commitment to my friend. I can exchange thoughts, ideas, and even secrets, and I know this person will hold them in trust. Friendship is a wonderful relationship, and I probably have very few true friends.

In my relationship with God, I find myself sharing my life with God, often conversing with God, being guided by the Spirit in the round of my life. I let the word find a home in my heart, and I manifest it in my ways of being in my home and my work. It prompts me to a concern for the world.

4. Another step in relationship is *intimacy*. Intimacy can occur between good friends or in a good marriage. Often words are not needed to communicate. Compared to our relationship with God one is simply in the presence of God without words or thoughts or images. One is simply in God's presence.

—Suzanne Toolan, RSM. These observations are adapted
from talks given by Fr. Thomas Keating.

Prison Ministry at San Quentin

I was in prison and you came to me.

—Matthew 25:36, RSV

The little beach town on the edge of the San Francisco Bay might be charming if it weren't for the shadow of a medieval-looking fortress whose crenellated towers loom near the cottages and the sandy streets. San Quentin State Prison has six thousand inmates and four thousand volunteers who visit them each year.

Sisters of Mercy archivist Sr. Marilyn Gouailhardou found a copy of a letter sent to *The Monitor* Catholic newspaper in 1894, expressing gratitude to the Sisters of Mercy who had been visiting San Quentin for forty years, since the Sisters had come to San Francisco in 1854. The Sisters also provided three hundred books for the library, which former archdiocesan detention minister Ray McKeon said were still there in 2006.

Sisters Suzanne and Marguerite have been among those going in and out through the sally ports, or security check points, for the last eight years. This forbidding place has drawn the two in part because of the loneliness of its inhabitants and the depth of its spiritual possibilities. Picking up the thread of prison visiting started by the first Sisters of Mercy to come to California, the two have brought Centering Prayer to the prisoners and in turn have been enriched by them. A faithful core of volunteers now visits every Monday.

Each time they go to San Quentin, Sisters Suzanne and Marguerite and the others park in the distant lot for visitors, walk to the fortress and show their driver's licenses to the guards. They are checked for weapons with a wand. Sr. Suzanne has to tell them each time that she has had metal knee and shoulder replacements that will set off the alarm.

The first time they visited the prison, they had to declare that they know they will not be rescued or ransomed if there is violence and they are held as hostages. So far that has not happened.

For each visit, they are ushered into the cage to wait for admission. The bars clank shut. As they are ushered out of the cage into the prison, they go quickly through the courtyard, past the rose-bushes to the chapel. On the left are the high windows of death row, grim and gimlet-eyed. Six hundred men are suspended here between this life and the next.

For Sr. Suzanne, Fr. Thomas Keating opened up the contemplative aspect of prayer in the early 1990s that had first drawn her to Taizé ten years before. Centering Prayer, a revival of the Christian contemplative tradition, emphasizes choosing a sacred word to renew the intention of remaining in God's presence. The word is not a mantra; it is a reminder. This discipline is simple: the goal is to bring people directly into the silence of God's presence and to consent to God's action.

It recalled Sr. Suzanne's lyrics for a hymn she had written in 1971:

> *Stilled and quiet is my soul.*
> *In God's presence I take my rest.* *

She felt at home with Centering Prayer. "The goal of Eastern meditation is enlightenment," explained Sr. Suzanne. "The goal of Christian meditation is union with God. Both lead to the same place. Centering Prayer is not a prayer of attention; it is a prayer of intention, an opening for God. You judge the quality of prayer not by the prayer

---

*"Stilled and Quiet," GIA copyright © 1966.

itself but by your life — if you find yourself to be more kind, more peaceful. You let others shine. You are less vengeful. You are more forgiving of yourself."

Sisters Suzanne and Marguerite went to St. Benedict's Monastery in Snowmass, Colorado, in 1996 to learn to teach the practice and afterward began to give workshops on it.

"Archdiocesan detention minister Ray McKeon asked us to talk to people who visit jails," remembered Suzanne, "to see if they would like to introduce this prayer. Some of them had visited jails for years and weren't that interested in doing something new. Then Ray asked us if we would consider San Quentin ourselves. So on October 4, 1998, ironically the day Fr. Thomas Keating came to Mercy Center to give a talk, Marguerite and I weren't there; we went to San Quentin to do a workshop on Centering Prayer.

"There were things I had to learn about teaching in prison. First, I said, 'You sit in a chair, so your back is straight.' Then I realized, for one thing, there are no chairs in the prison cells. We started the next Monday and went every Monday to the prison for the next two years." Although they have taught the prayer at Mercy Center, they have found an intimate prayer group at San Quentin.

Centering Prayer requires daily quiet time, which is not easy in prison. There is constant noise, often violence, work, and some classes, all of which occupy and distract the men. How do they get quiet time? Jeff, a gray-haired man in his sixties, with a smooth face, eyes hooded by heavy lids, and a warm smile, said, yes, in the afternoons there is time.* Another gets up at 3:30 a.m. before reporting to work at 4:30 a.m.

"If you've been down [in prison] a long time you get set in your ways," Jeff said. "You are quiet some of the time." His celly [cell mate] is quiet a lot. There is also time after lights out. "You have all night then," he said.

---

*The men's names have all been changed.

Justin has been one of the steady ones over the years in San Quentin who has found "doing time" is a unique gift. "After Vatican II, I left the Church. Things that were 'always the same' had changed. It wasn't until I got to prison that I had a real experience of God. It was an experience of light. The intensity of the experience of the Holy Spirit was so much that I said, 'It's too much!' It happened twice. Now I can't say that my prayer is just important to me; I can't live without it." Sr. Suzanne has kept a brief diary about these men and their Monday-night meetings. Henry, for example, is a wise, self-reflective man, almost a saint in his way, although he probably murdered someone to get in there. Larry is from a local parish and has been in prison many times, each time resolving to stay out, a frequent scenario for many. When Ignacio is released he will be deported immediately to Indonesia, so release is not entirely welcome.

Sr. Suzanne often begins a description of an inmate with "There is this darling guy," although she knows he has been and could still be violent. She talks about San Quentin with a deep concern, even tenderness. Leading the men in an evening of Centering Prayer is an opportunity to reach out to the very poor and downtrodden of the world. She believes in the potential for each one, although they have great obstacles to staying out of prison without intense rehabilitation and support.

The chapel at San Quentin is large, with bare white walls and wooden Stations of the Cross. The Sisters talk with the men informally before the prayer begins. They have gotten to know them, although the prisoners come and go. Sometimes the Sisters and other volunteers can't come because the prisoners are on lockdown as a result of an incident in the prison, and they are unable to come out of their cells to the chapel.

The numbers vary; sometimes a discouragingly small group assembles. There are many other classes and activities in the evenings that compete with Centering Prayer when there are not lockdowns. When the Sisters began Centering Prayer, the men and volunteers began by sitting in a circle for a twenty-minute session of quiet. Sr. Suzanne felt that something wasn't really working, although they were at a loss to discover what it was.

"It took us a long time to arrive at a structure," she said. "It was when Marguerite suggested a ten-minute walk followed by a second twenty-minute sitting that the sessions really began to work. Two men had been at Folsom Prison where there is a large contemplative group, and we asked them to help us. They said we needed quiet music and a bell."

The men now play quiet music to make a break from their chaotic lives in prison. Then they ring a bell and begin their period of prayer and walking. Then they talk about the role of Centering Prayer in their lives and end with lectio divina, a prayerful reading of Scripture.

At one session, Sisters Suzanne and Marguerite asked, Is it possible to find beauty at San Quentin? "The sharing was great, "said Sr. Suzanne. Here are some of her notes from that session in 2000:

Ignacio said that he likes to see every person there as a human and therefore beautiful.

Henry said that there are such diverse men there, members of gangs, homosexuals, a man who goes around with a red cape. He says that he sees beauty in them all and tries to relate with them in this way. He gave a homosexual a hug despite what other men thought. There was a man who went around picking up cigarette butts. (It was the man's birthday.) Henry told him not to do that but to come by his cell before lockdown. He gave him a pouch of tobacco and said, "Happy Birthday."

Lloyd says that he has known Henry for a long time and has been so inspired by his growth.

*Bob said that you had to watch out, to be on guard because
you never know how people were going to be. But he says that
he sees beauty in the sky, the roses around the chapel area.*

Sr. Mary Ann Scofield, who also visits San Quentin for Centering
Prayer, remarked that one man told her that not many people on
the outside have the luxury of the time "to get your head together"
as he does here. "You're just too busy on the outside," he told her.

"At San Quentin, God is what they have to hold on to," observed volunteer Carol Fowler who also teaches Centering Prayer
with Sr. Suzanne. "They look at life through the prism of relationship with God. When they get together to pray, there isn't any other
motivation than to be alone and to experience prayer with others.
I've seen the transforming effect Centering Prayer has had. They
have hit rock bottom. What they experience with God is inner peace
and tremendous joy."

Carol observed, "This San Quentin group is Suzanne's prayer
group. It's a real gift for Suzanne in her busy life to be able to go
to pray there."

Going to San Quentin gave Sisters Suzanne and Marguerite
the inspiration to fill another need — taking Taizé prayer to the
women's prison across the San Francisco Bay in Dublin. Resourceful
and persistent, Sr. Marguerite found the opportunity. The trip is not
a simple proposition. Monthly they load everything into the car —
keyboard, Taizé cross, candles, altar cloth, and drive across the bay
to a group of mostly Hispanic women. A large group of volunteers,
some of whom can speak Spanish, are equally dedicated.

"We do a hodgepodge of a service," said Sr. Suzanne. "We read
Scripture and invite them to talk about how it relates to their lives.
We have silence — our nod to Centering Prayer — and then Taizé
prayer. During Taizé, they each stay a long time at the cross, laying
down heavy burdens. There is much weeping, and some kind soul
brings toilet paper to help with the tears. No tissues are furnished

in prison. We can't hug them, but we've recently established that a 'ritual hug' during the service is OK."

Her prison visits have been a satisfying outgrowth of Suzanne's own prayer life. "Prison ministry is really working with the marginalized," she said. "There is always a lack in us if we don't have the privilege of working with the marginalized."

Directly out of her prayer came Sr. Suzanne's idea for a local center for women leaving prison. She and Marguerite had seen directly how difficult it is for people to stay out of prison once there because of the lack of support for felons once they leave.

"The idea came to me when I was meditating in our chapel one morning. I thought, 'I'll ask Lillian [Sr. Lillian Murphy, CEO of Mercy Housing, who lives in Denver, Colorado]. As I left, Lillian happened to be in the corridor!"

Sr. Lillian was interested, but Mercy Housing wasn't able to help shelter the women. Sr. Suzanne's idea gathered steam. Under Sr. Marguerite's leadership, a transitional house including shelter and programs for six women at a time has become a dynamic reality. Suzanne created a daily meditation for them for a year. Catherine's Center, sponsored by the Society of St. Vincent de Paul, now has guided many women out of prison and into productive lives. As an indication of its success, the Society of St. Vincent de Paul increased the space to accommodate ten women altogether.

In January 2006, Catherine's Center held an event that honored Sr. Suzanne for its founding inspiration and for her music. Many Mercy High graduates who had been in her chorale came to honor her. The service included the San Francisco Schola Cantorum's performance of Suzanne's setting of Gerard Manley Hopkins's poem "God's Grandeur." The response was overwhelming. Over four hundred people came to pay tribute to Sr. Suzanne, double the usual number for this annual fundraiser. One alumna said, "It's about time someone honored her!"

The event ended with a dramatic symbolic gesture that illustrated the spreading of Sr. Suzanne's inspired spark. The women
from Catherine's Center and the center's supporters, many of whom
were chorale members, processed out of the dark chapel carrying
candles—a blending of the two streams of experiences and talents
out into the world.

While she was at Mercy Center, Sr. Suzanne didn't feel that
the programs then effectively reached the poor. The staff made
many efforts, but the barriers of distance and culture prevented
their success in consistently reaching the most economically
needy at that time. In prison ministry and at Catherine's Center,
Sr. Suzanne, Sr. Marguerite, and their volunteers have continually
closed the circle, giving refreshment and encouragement to those
who hunger and thirst. The hungry and thirsty ones have given
back, often with a deep experience of prayer and the courage to
grow in their life of God no matter what the circumstances.

CENTERING PRAYER IN PRISON
BY DANIEL J. COSTA

Daniel had returned to prison five times in twenty years. Despite his sincere efforts to change, the old patterns returned. He discovered Centering Prayer at San Quentin Prison and realized that transformation from the inside, not just in the exterior actions of his life, was essential.

With the encouragement of my new friend, Kenny, I decided to give Centering Prayer a chance at transforming what I previously believed was untransformable — my life! I began Centering Prayer at San Quentin's Catholic chapel, facilitated by George Biniek, Sisters Suzanne Toolan, and Marguerite Buchanan. I was instructed in the methodology, but what caught my attention was the lack of reference to anything outside of my life.

The focus was on the inside, an inward journey, seeking God's Divine Presence within me, a contact as a result of responding to the Spirit of Christ by consenting to God's presence and action within. Once this contact was made, God would take care of the rest. There was nothing further for me to do.

When you photograph someone, the image of that person is imprinted onto the photographic film or plate inside the camera once the external light hits the plate. The photographic plate then goes into a "darkroom" for development. The plate is slid into a special chemical solution in order for the imprinted image to become visible through this transformative process. Similarly, in the process of spiritual transformation, the Christian enters his "secret room" (Matt. 6:6) and with the light of intellectual understanding turned off, allows his soul to slide into the "divine solution" of God's Presence. It is through the vehicle of Centering Prayer that the imprinted image of Christ develops and becomes visible in our everyday lives. Through Centering Prayer, each session is an opportunity to encounter Christ and allow Him to be "magnified in my body" (Phil. 1:20, KJV).

I believe that if we are ever to see the Christlike characteristics of a love for one's enemies, a joy that is not at the mercy of favorable conditions, a peace that surpasses all understanding, a patience that endures long-suffering, a kindness that takes no offense, a generosity toward those in need, a faith that can move mountains, a gentleness that softens the most hardened sinner, and a self-control that leaves one free to be more receptive to the needs of others (Gal. 5:22–23, RSV), it is through Centering Prayer and time spent in "God's darkroom" that we encounter and will be transformed by our union with Christ Jesus. This the only way; this is God's Way.

A Community of Freedom

Sr. Suzanne stands at the heavy oak door at the end of a corridor and enters a code onto the raised keypad numbers. The latch clicks open in the shadows. By this time, she's forgotten the irony: the doors of the Mercy Motherhouse have been locked against intruders only since 2002, but in many ways they have never been more open.

The rigid confines of the old habit, metaphorical and literal, and an hourly pattern of prayer and work are gone. Sr. Suzanne, in her soft full skirts and cardigan with her crepe-soled black sandals, comes and goes freely through the convent doors, as do her Sisters who live here. The doors mark the area of their private lives, set off from Mercy Center, which hosts visitors year round.

In spite of the freedom, many have moved out of this Motherhouse, where all those who have entered the Burlingame region of the Sisters of Mercy since 1931 have come for formation and training. Perhaps the long corridors notched by small bedrooms and the cavernous dining room were too impersonal. Hungering for a separate adult identity, many Sisters moved into apartments or into shared houses in the early 1990s. About thirty remain, living in small community groups or independently in the house.

Sr. Suzanne stayed, partly out of simple loyalty but more out of love for the community of her Sisters and for the work she continues to do here. Her office, just off the chapel but behind the locked door, contains the basics of her life: desk, aging computer in its turquoise shell, telephone, and upright piano. A gently worn, brocaded love seat rescued from a parlor redecoration greets visitors.

A photo of Sr. Suzanne flanked by her natural sisters Pat and Mary Louise, all laughing and in full habit, sits on a corner shelf; another of them as children rests on her file cabinet. In the soft, natural light of the room, a Taizé cross hangs on one wall and the face of Christ, the art for her latest album, is framed on another.

The small living group of teachers that Sr. Marguerite and Sr. Suzanne formed in the 1970s has evolved into the Montsalvat Community with five core members and at least seven adjunct members who all live in the Motherhouse. The core members say evening prayer together before eating dinner in their own dining room. As a group they celebrate each others' feast days with gifts, cards, and a special meal. Evenings in their community room, some (including Sr. Suzanne) play often boisterous card games of "Hand and Foot," driving some of the quieter members out of the room.

The Burlingame Sisters have always had good parties — inventive skits, home-grown, stand-up comedy routines, and songs written for the occasion. Sr. Suzanne's "pianologs," which captured personalities of Sisters in music, are fondly remembered.

Friday and Sunday nights in Montsalvat — wine, cheese, and evening prayer — draw Sisters together. Adjunct members, who live elsewhere in the Motherhouse, and visiting Sisters are welcomed to warm themselves in the glow of community.

The group enjoys its collective memories of joint domestic adventures. "We have cooked Thanksgiving dinner together," remembered Sr. Suzanne. "One year after the dinner, Sr. Mary Clement blithely made Irish coffee with strong real coffee and added coffee crystals. None of us slept that night. We found each other up doing work, typing away at 2:00 a.m. Then there was the time she melted the knobs on the oven by accidentally broiling instead of baking a cake."

"When I was facilitating Taizé prayer all over the [San Francisco] Bay Area every night of Lent," said Suzanne, "Sisters Edna Dorsett and Marie Meller would wait up for me with hot chocolate and ask eagerly, 'How did it go?' Everyone is always so happy and proud of each other."

The women who enter the Mercy religious life today don't find "the boundaries of the bell" or a monitored schedule. The responsibility for interior growth is individual. Sr. Suzanne and her sisters tread their own paths in a dance of aloneness and community.

"We had an exterior structure," said Sr. Marguerite, "but now you have to find your own interior structure. Finding our own pattern was so liberating for each of us. We learned various ways of praying and nurturing our life in God."

"We still have Eucharist in the morning and evening prayer," said Sr. Suzanne, who leads early morning meditation for people in the convent and retreat center and faithful neighbors outside the Motherhouse as well. "Annual, weeklong retreats are very important to us."

The religious life which she loved from her entrance flourishes, not as a group of women sitting in rows, but as circles of individuals, each with her own opinion. Circles require discussion, consensus, and time. Few decisions come down from the top. The process of deciding who should be in leadership or what work should be sponsored by the community is often laborious. The opening of Mercy Center in 1982 came as a result of this careful process.

Sr. Suzanne leads her Mercy community and the larger Church by her prayerful presence and by constant contributions of her music. The National Association of Pastoral Musicians gave her their highest honor, the Jubilate Deo Award in 1998 for her lifetime contribution to liturgy and music.

As the choral conductor John Renke said of her, "People most successful in religious life don't fit into a mold. They understand how to draw on religious life to be themselves." Sr. Suzanne has drawn on the strengths of religious community and reflected them back through the prism of her talents. Her star has been bright, lighting the way for contemporary music and prayer.

Reflection Questions

This set of reflection questions is limited to topics that we felt were most beneficial to those interested in liturgy and music. They are therefore oriented around six topics which do correspond to those pertinent essays.

Questions for Reflection: Silence
1. Are there repetitive physical things that you do where you are naturally silent? Can you become more aware of the healing quality of this silence? (Examples: knitting, gardening, walking, painting.)
2. In the liturgy of which you are a part, does silence help people to absorb the message and pray?
3. If people in your parish are uncomfortable with silence, are there gradual ways you can introduce it to them?

Questions for Reflection: Liturgy
1. What could you do to increase the sense of natural flow to your liturgy?
2. What does Sr. Suzanne's statement that "liturgy ... is a form, a vessel" mean to you?
3. What do you think are the strongest elements of the liturgy you help prepare?

Questions for Reflection: Ritual
1. Does understanding that the liturgy is a ritual make a difference in how you approach liturgy?

2. What are some rituals that are a part of your own family history?

3. Are there personal rituals you have discovered are helpful in your life as you mark the passage from one segment of your life to another?

Questions for Reflection: Articulating Belief

1. Think about your favorite hymns. Are they strong? What message do they convey? Do they help people pray?

2. How do you help the assembly to be comfortable with new music?

3. Think about the larger message that the music you choose sends: old familiar pieces, contemporary favorites, guitar-accompanied songs, songs led by a cantor or sung by a choir, new works, sad songs at funerals. Are you intending these messages?

Questions for Reflection: Symbols

1. Are the major symbols of Eucharist very evident in the architecture of your church, the appointments of the church? Can you do more to highlight them?

2. Can symbols change? Can something that was a symbol become outdated?

3. Can you think of art objects used in the liturgy of which you are a part that you might think of as "failed" symbols?

Questions for Reflection: Environment

1. Do you agree with the distinction between entertainment and enchantment?

2. Can you visualize ways to involve but not overwhelm the senses for a liturgy in your space?

3. Do you ask people in your parish to take responsibility for what happens during liturgy?

4. Do you think Sr. Suzanne's standards can apply to multicultural congregations?

Glossary

Baldachino: A canopy over an altar.

Charism: The special purpose or mission of a religious community.

Coif: A white covering over the head under a nun's black veil.

Dialogue Mass or **missa recitata:** A Mass which allows a liturgical conversation between the presider and the congregation.

Final vows: Vows made for life committing oneself to God and to a religious community.

First-class days: Days that were part of the celebration of first-class feast days, such as Christmas, Easter, Ascension, and the Assumption. On these days, the religious community celebrated by allowing talking among the women and often enjoyed special festive meals. Second-class feast days were celebrations of feast days of major saints, such as St. Peter or St. Catherine.

Formation: A period of study and prayer during which a novice or a woman with temporary vows learns the expectations of the community and through guidance deepens her own spiritual life.

Guimpe: The white cloth that covered the shoulders in a sister's habit.

Horarium: The daily schedule of the community.

Novice: The next step after postulancy, lasting two years.

Ordinary Time: The days of the liturgical calendar that are not part of the major seasons of the church year. Ordinary time occurs in winter and again after Pentecost, in late spring through fall.

Ostinato: A phrase repeated throughout a piece. Especially used in Taizé prayer.

Postulant: One who has been accepted into formation for a religious community. The period of postulancy was six months. The women wore black dresses (not yet habits), which differentiated them from the vowed members of the community. Today women who have declared their interest in the community and have been accepted for a period of trial are called candidates.

Temporary vows: Vows taken for a year at a time for a period of three years.

Triduum: The three-day period of the church year that begins with Holy Thursday and ends with Easter Sunday. It is the holiest period of the church year in its celebration of the passion, death, and resurrection of Christ.

Acknowledgments

From Sr. Suzanne Toolan

I would like to acknowledge my gratitude to my family. We are a strange lot in many ways: we inherited the thrift of the Germans and the humor of the Irish. I can't imagine a better family in which to be born.

The Sisters of Mercy have been a nurturing ground for a strong desire for God, for prayer. They have always appreciated me more than I deserve.

I thank each student I have ever taught. I loved precious moments standing in front of a choir, together sculpting sound that was sometimes awful and sometimes way beyond ourselves.

I thank Liz Dossa who came to my office once a week with a notebook and put me so much at ease that I found myself just telling my story.

From Elizabeth Dossa

I am grateful especially to Sr. Suzanne Toolan. Enduring the spotlight is difficult for her, so it was with grace that she tolerated sharing personal materials — old programs, talks, unpublished pieces, reflections and photos — and talking about her life with me.

I am indebted to:

Sr. Marguerite Buchanan, RSM, who graciously read the manuscript and gave suggestions;

Sr. Marilyn Gouailhardou, RSM, community archivist, who supplied helpful comments and allowed me access to the Mercy Community's historical materials;

Catherine Murphy, former student of Sr. Suzanne's, who helped me broaden my understanding of recent Church history;

Suzanne Buckley, Director of Mercy Center, whose enthusiasm and ideas moved me forward;

The Sisters of Mercy leadership, Sr. Mary Waskowiak, RSM; the late Sr. Diane Grassilli, RSM; Sr. Anne Murphy, RSM; Sr. Ellene Egan, RSM; and Sr. Sherry Dolan, RSM, who were enthusiastic about having Sr. Suzanne's story told; and especially Sr. Carolyn Krohn, RSM, who encouraged me with the idea of writing about Sr. Suzanne from its very beginning;

So many people — Sr. Suzanne's colleagues, former students and Mercy Sisters — who freely gave of their memories of her;

Editorial consultant Roy M. Carlisle, who helped the shape the book, steering me gently in fruitful directions and sending notes of encouragement at key moments along the path.

My husband, Al, who put up with my so often being in front of a computer and who also believed in the value of telling Sr. Suzanne's story.

About the Authors

Gloria Ernestine Toolan was born in Lansing, Michigan, in 1927. The family moved to Hollywood, California, when Gloria was seventeen years old. There she studied organ with Richard Keys Biggs and became his assistant organist at St. Paul's Church in Los Angeles. She became choir director and organist at St. Ambrose Church in Hollywood while still playing organ at St. Paul's. Her initiation into choral work (her great love), was through Lucianne Gourdon Biggs, with whom she apprenticed at St. Paul's Church and at Villa Cabrini Academy in Burbank.

After completing a Bachelor of Arts degree at Immaculate Heart College in Hollywood, Gloria entered the Sisters of Mercy in Burlingame, California, in 1950. She subsequently did composition course work at Michigan State University, liturgical study at the University of Notre Dame, and choral work with Robert Shaw at San Diego State University. She received her MA from San Francisco State University.

Sr. Suzanne became a teacher at Mercy High School in Burlingame, where she taught choral music and became a team member for an extended campus alternative program where students explored the Bay Area resources in arts and sciences.

Under Sr. Suzanne's direction, Mercy's prize-winning choirs sang throughout the Bay Area for both religious and civic events. Writing music for her choirs and for the groups with whom she worked became an important part of her ministry. It was during this time that the Roman Catholic Church was in need of repertory in the vernacular. Sr. Suzanne enthusiastically joined the ranks of those who were trying to fill the void.

In 1981, while still continuing with some high school teaching, Sr. Suzanne became the first director of Mercy Center in Burlingame. From the beginning the Center became a place of openness and welcome. The Center, under subsequent leadership, has become internationally known and respected.

For almost thirty years the prayer and music of Taizé has been an important part of Suzanne's life. She has led the prayer is many parts of the United States and has modeled many of her own compositions on the prayerful style of this ecumenical community

Elizabeth Dossa is director of communications for the Burlingame Regional Community of the Sisters of Mercy. She has written articles on Sisters, spirituality, art and music over the last twenty years for *U.S. Catholic, Strings* magazine, *Stanford* magazine, and other magazines and newspapers, both Catholic and secular. She began working with the Sisters of Mercy as an English teacher at Mercy High School in Burlingame in 1980. A graduate of Pomona College, she received her Master of Arts in teaching at the Harvard School of Education and a Certificate of Arts Administration from Golden Gate University.

With Sr. Amy Bayley and with the encouragement of Sr. Suzanne Toolan she founded Music at Kohl Mansion, a chamber music series in Burlingame in 1982 based in the original Mercy High School building. After working with the series for ten years, she left to join the Peninsula Symphony as its executive director. The Peninsula Symphony, made up of community players dedicated to music, was a delightful grassroots experience of working with people who truly have a love affair with the arts.

She returned to the Sisters of Mercy campus in 1997 to work in communications for the Sisters throughout California and Arizona. She has felt privileged to witness their lives as women religious from the vantage of a staff person and to feel their spiritual resourcefulness, organizational skill, and compassionate community, especially as they face the facts of shrinking numbers.

She and her husband, Al, have three grown daughters.

Of Related Interest

Suzanne Buckley, ed.
SACRED IS THE CALL
Formation and Transformation
in Spiritual Direction Programs

"*Sacred Is the Call* is a treasure with layers and layers of
wisdom and insight." — *Benedictines* Book Reviews

Mercy Center, a leading spiritual direction program in the
United States, presents *Sacred Is the Call,* edited by Suzanne
Buckley, Director of Mercy Center. By presenting the twenty
key topics for spiritual direction training by the top experts in
the field and also providing wise guidance for seekers looking
for spiritual transformation, this handbook fulfills its promise
as *the* text for spiritual directors and trainers. Topics include contemplative listening, discernment, the wisdom of the
body, sexuality, prayer, gender issues, justice concerns, group
spiritual direction, psychology in spiritual direction, formation guidelines, and many others. Each contribution features
reflection questions and suggestions for further reading.

0-8245-2338-5, paperback

Check your local bookstore for availability.
To order directly from the publisher,
please call 1-800-707-0670 for Customer Service
or visit our Web site at *www.cpcbooks.com.*
For catalog orders, please send your request to the address below.

THE CROSSROAD PUBLISHING COMPANY
16 Penn Plaza, Suite 1550
New York, NY 10001

crossroad